101

Best of Tunney
Side of Sports Columns

Dr. Jim Tunney
"Dean of NFL Referees"

ISBN: 978-1-60679-301-5
Library of Congress Control Number: 2014931887
Book layout: Cheery Sugabo
Cover design: Cheery Sugabo
Front cover image: iStock/Thinkstock

Coaches Choice
P.O. Box 1828
Monterey, CA 93942
www.coacheschoice.com

Dedication

First and foremost is my gratitude to my wife, Linda, for the countless hours she allowed me to spend in my "man cave" each week while writing these articles. Her patience and understanding was beyond my wildest expectations. I love you!

Further, I dedicate these writings to my family and friends who read the many columns/blogs and have offered their wisdom and comments.

Acknowledgments

Words of gratitude pale in comparison for my true feelings of gratitude for John Oldach, an independent editing and writing professional, for his expertise in the edits and review of the content and context of these writings.

My appreciation as well goes to Dr. Jim Peterson and his great team at Coaches Choice for their wonderful collaborative efforts in making this book a reality.

Foreword

Sports have always been a part of Jim Tunney's life. As a kid, you could find him on the local playground every day after school, and growing up in Southern California he was able to play every day. This book was formed from that background.

In high school and college, he played the major sports—football, basketball, and baseball. At Occidental College, he played all three and, as a senior, was voted athlete-of-the-year. As a senior, he was selected to coach the college freshman baseball team, which he led to a 23-2 winning season and a league championship. Teaching and coaching at the high school level was always his ambition, and he was fortunate to receive a job upon graduation from Oxy. The high school basketball teams he coached won two league championships in his four-year coaching career, with his final year resulting in an undefeated season (1955)—the school's record today.

Jim's 30-year career as an educator saw him principal of three large inner-city high schools, mostly during the turbulent 1960s. Some years after his successful principalship at Fairfax High School (Los Angeles), he was honored to be that school's first administrator to be inducted into their Alumni Hall of Fame. Leaving LAUSD, he was selected as superintendent of a school district just outside of Los Angeles. He earned a doctorate from the University of Southern California during his tenure as a high school principal.

His 31-year NFL career set a standard for officiating in the National Football League. He was honored by being assigned 29 post-season officiating assignments which included 3 Super Bowls, 10 championship games, 6 Pro Bowls, and 25 Monday night games, when MNF was THE game of the week. He was the youngest to referee a Super Bowl game (VI) and followed that with back-to-back Super Bowls (XI and XII), being the only referee to work consecutive Super Bowls. His picture in the NFL rule book depicting officials' signals appeared there for 19 years.

Moreover his ability as a leader is noted with his history of being elected president or chair of the board of every organization to which he belonged. Most noteworthy of these are: NASO (National Association of Sports Officials), which honored him with its gold whistle award; PFRA (Professional Football [NFL] Referees Association); and NSA (National Speakers Association).

Speaking of NSA, Jim holds every honor and designation that organization awards including the NSA Speaker Hall of Fame and the Cavett (the "Oscar" of professional speaking) as well as the Philanthropist of the Year. His philanthropic work is outstanding. In 1993 he created the Jim Tunney Youth Foundation to provide funding for the youth in his community to develop their leadership, work skills, self-esteem, and wellness. To date JTYF has contributed over a quarter million dollars to that effort.

His twelve-year tenure as a publicly elected community college trustee saw him chair of that college board for six of those years. One of his defining contributions was involving the community to pass a major bond measure to rebuild its aging campus. He was honored to receive the College President's Award as well as the Chamber of Commerce Public Official of the Year.

As a writer he has authored or co-authored nine books. This book *101 Best of Tunney Side of Sports Columns* is his tenth. His co-authored *Chicken Soup for the Sports Fan's Soul* was on the *New York Times* best seller list for three weeks and has sold nearly a million copies. He continues to write a weekly newspaper column bearing the title of this book and is approaching his 500th column.

I am confident you will learn, laugh, and be a better person reading the stories in this book.

—Jim Nantz

Jim Nantz has been in sports broadcasting over 35 years. He is currently "The Voice of CBS" as its lead announcer for NFL games, the NCAA basketball's Final Four, and the PGA tour including the Masters, which he has hosted consecutively since 1989. An Emmy-winning sports personality, Dr. Nantz was awarded an honorary doctorate in humane letters from the University of Houston, his alma mater.

Preface

It was my Speakers Roundtable colleagues at our 2005 meeting that provided the impetus for these Tunney Side articles/blogs. I have been writing a weekly newspaper column ever since. At first the column was to be called "On the Tunney Side of the Street"—a play on that old standard "On the Sunny Side of the Street," you know, "grab your coat, get your hat, leave your worries on the doorstep, life can be—" well, you get the picture. That title morphed into "On the Tunney Side of Sports." It is the belief here that sports issues—good/bad/right or wrong can prove to be positive examples for everyday living. The major emphasis of these articles is to take sports issues and transform them into positive messages to help others lead productive lives. I am confident that you will find a story in here that can make a difference in your personal and/or professional life. Now, it is up to you to make your life more fun, healthier, and more productive. Will you do it?

Contents

1 ATTITUDE

August 20, 2007

After further review …

What made Bill Walsh so special? Coach Bill Walsh died July 30, 2007 after a battle with leukemia. Bill was the coach of the San Francisco 49ers from 1979 to 1988. During that time, he won three Super Bowls (XVI, XIX, and XXIII), six NFC Championships, and had a record of 102 wins and 63 losses. Although he was often referred to as the "genius" because of his innovative, creative football thinking, his depth went beyond football.

The specialness to which I am referring was the "man" inside the head of the genius. That term—genius—incidentally, made Coach Walsh uncomfortable. He thought of himself not only as a football coach, but as a builder of men. Just weeks before his death, he said, "I'd like to get all the men I have coached together. That would be special." On August 9, 2007, all his "men" did just that by being at Stanford University Chapel to pay homage to him.

Walsh's successful career is not without its difficulties. I first met Bill when he was an assistant to Paul Brown, head coach and founder of the Cincinnati Bengals. The Bengals played, and lost, to the Oakland Raiders in a divisional playoff game in 1974. I was the referee. The next year, Paul Brown stepped aside and most football experts thought Bill would get the Bengals' head coaching job. He didn't. It bothered him so much he left the Bengals to take an assistant coaching job with the San Diego Chargers.

As an NFL referee, I was on the field every year throughout Coach Walsh's career. I also had the privilege of giving rules talks to the Niners, and sat in team meetings watching that left-hander diagram plays and discussing rules. Bill was a student of the rules and would often debate rule interpretations. To my knowledge, he never did anything to circumvent the rulebook.

After Bill retired, we became friends; we played golf and visited at social and athletic functions. That usually doesn't happen in the world of NFL officials, but I then saw in Bill what his players knew all along. Often, when we were together, someone would come up to say hello. Bill would always introduce himself by saying, "Hi, I'm Bill Walsh," as if this visitor didn't know who he was.

His humility and lack of self-aggrandizement typified the kind of man he was. Someone once said of him, "Bill Walsh didn't know he was Bill Walsh," a tribute that epitomizes this man.

 Will you walk in footprints left by Bill Walsh?

June 30, 2008

After further review …

You want drama, perseverance, courage, and a "no quit" attitude? Try the 108th U.S. Open at Torrey Pines. How about adding a fun, pleasant attitude? As a major PGA Championship like the U.S. Open? Exactly.

If you watched the first three rounds—Thursday, Friday, and Saturday—there wasn't much fun being tossed around on the golf course. In fact, when Tiger Woods was coupled with Phil Mickelson (along with Adam Scott), pleasantries seemed to be missing. Phil always seemed to have a smile on his face, but Tiger is so focused that he rarely smiles at or recognizes his competitor. It's not that he's unpleasant—just focused.

But did you recognize what 45-year-old Rocco Mediate brought to the Monday playoff after Tiger tied him on Sunday? A pleasant, fun attitude—"What do I have to lose," Rocco said. Refreshing. Then in the playoff, *both* he and Tiger exchanged pleasantries throughout the match. "Obviously, I would have loved to win, but it was great fun," said Rocco in post-game interviews. Was Rocco focused? Of course. Yet, he treated this highly competitive event, *the* U.S. Open, with the joy of just being able to play it. As important as the Open is—it's still just a *game*.

There's a story about a man who moves into a small town and stops at a gas station. When the attendant approaches (yes, they used to have attendants at "service stations"), the stranger says, "I just moved here. How are the people in this town to get along with?" The attendant responds by asking him how the people were in the town the stranger just left. "Terrible," says the stranger. "Impolite, harsh, and uncaring." The attendant says, "Well, you'll find them that way here, too."

About that time, another man pulls into the station right near the first guy and says to the attendant, "I just moved here. How are the people that live here?" The attendant asks, "Well, how were the people in the town you just left?" "Wonderful," says the second man. "Friendly, cared about you, honest, and all that." The attendant replies, "Well, you'll find them that way here, too."

The first man says to the attendant, "Wait a minute, you didn't tell *me* that." The attendant replies, "Well, people usually respond the way you interact with them." Rocco interacted in a fun, enjoyable way to Tiger, and Tiger responded in like manner.

 Will you present a positive, caring attitude toward others?

After further review …

Burl Toler, Sr. was a National Football League game official for 25 years. He carried #37 on the back of his NFL officiating jersey. More than that, he carried himself, both on and off the field, with grace and dignity. Burl died on August 16, 2009, and I not only lost a fellow official, but a good friend.

Burl worked as a head linesman in a crew where I was privileged to serve as his crew chief in the on-field position as referee. We worked in the same crew for 11 consecutive seasons. When two officials are together every Saturday and Sunday for 11 seasons, you become family. Burl and I were just that.

It may be difficult for some to imagine what it is like to be a black man (you may prefer African American) putting on an NFL official's uniform that no other of his race had done. Burl was the first black NFL official when he joined our ranks in 1965. There were black players and assistant coaches, but only a few. There were some racial animosities between players in the early 1960s, and maybe some "concern" whether a black man could officiate an NFL game.

That was never an issue with Burl Toler. He had earned the right to wear those stripes. Burl was an outstanding linebacker at the University of San Francisco, playing on a USF T.E.A.M. that sent 11 players to the NFL, including Gino Marchetti, Bob St. Clair, and Ollie Mattson. Mattson and Toler were the only two black players on that undefeated 1951 Dons team (9-0), with the team being invited to two Bowl games. They—the Dons—turned down those invitations because "blacks weren't allowed to go with the team."

Turning down those Bowl invitations was a touching moment for Toler and Mattson, and, I believe, developed a personal strength for Burl as he pursued a career in officiating. Burl was a teacher at Ben Franklin Junior High School and eventually became its principal. Franklin Junior High became Ben Franklin Middle School, and then became Burl A. Toler Middle School. To receive the recognition of having a school named in your honor has to be the epitome of the grace, dignity, and service of the man.

In the 25 years Burl served as an on-field official, including Super Bowl XIV where he was—again—the first black official to work a Super Bowl, his presence dignified the position.

 Will you handle unkind remarks with a "Toler-kind" of attitude?

April 26, 2010

After further review …

The theme of a business conference to which I am invited as the keynote speaker is "Doing the Right Things." Certainly, the attendees—the best in their field—did the right things to get to the top of their profession. Being skilled in your job merits recognition. However, are you willing to do things right (meaning ethically), as well as doing the right things?

The question was answered emphatically in the Verizon Heritage Golf Tournament playoff recently. Golf professional Brian Davis sank an 18-foot putt on the final round to get into a tie with the (then) leader Jim Furyk. Davis and Furyk then went to the 18th tee for the playoff.

Both drives were in the middle of the fairway with Davis' ball being "away." Davis' approach shot went left, bounced off the green, then into the sand—a placed called Calibogue Sound. The ball, while playable, settled among some reeds and twigs. Furyk hit his approach shot onto the green.

Although Davis' ball lay off the green, Furyk was away and putted first to about four feet from the pin. Davis, after careful consideration, hit his shot onto the green, but then hesitated as he climbed out of the Calibogue Sound and summoned the rules official. What was Davis doing? Well, it seemed that "out of the corner of my eye," Davis had brushed a loose twig, in violation of rule 13.4—"moving a loose impediment during take-away," but no one saw that violation—except Davis.

Davis called the foul on himself and "after further review" (of the TV replay), the rules official concurred—"Violation 2-stroke penalty." Davis now lies 4 with Furyk lying 3. Davis concedes. Furyk putts for par, wins the Verizon Heritage and $1,026,000. Davis, in second place, gets $615,000—a difference of $411,000. Davis called the violation on himself. Is integrity worth $411,000?

Would an NFL wide receiver who just caught the winning touchdown pass as time expired come back to the referee and say, "Excuse me, but I pushed that defensive back before I caught the pass, so take away that touchdown?" Or an NBA player intercepts the ball, breaks away, and scores the winning basket as time expires. However, he blatantly "travelled" so he asks the referee to disregard his winning shot and lose the game?

Are you kidding me? Never would happen. Was Davis' self-penalizing gesture one of sportsmanship? Maybe. More importantly, it was an act of character.

 Will you respect the rules in the game of life with a Davis attitude in mind?

October 25, 2010

After further review …

The author of a book I read recently used the term "confident expectancy," described as: expect things to happen or change in your favor. It is based on faith and believing in yourself. I like that. Of course, that concept is not new.

We all know legendary and inspiration gurus, e.g., Napoleon Hill (*Think and Grow Rich*), Norman Vincent Peale (*Power of Positive Thinking*), Earl Nightingale, Og Mandino, Zig Ziglar, Tony Robbins, and Wayne Dyer. Many of my speaker roundtable colleagues (www.speakersroundtable.com) work with people in companies, associations, and organizations expressing the philosophy: "What you can conceive and believe, you can achieve."

However, asking the aforementioned question, "What is your level of expectancy," is inappropriate. There can be no levels. The "level" must be at 100 percent. Self-doubt in any small degree creates a wall of fear that you won't be successful. "I don't think I can do that" or "I'll probably fail" are words that easily pop into one's mind. The poem on my wall says something like this: *If you think you can't, you won't; if you think you can, you will. Success comes to the one who thinks he/she can.*

Now that doesn't mean if you have never high jumped in a track and field event, you can start by exceeding the world record. No high jumper in history ever started that way. But as you achieve one height, you then set your goal to exceed that. It grows from there.

I watched Dwight Stones, Olympic high jumper and one time world record holder, preparing to jump at an event. He closed his eyes for a minute or so, and then began his approach to jump. I asked afterward what he was doing in that minute of preparation. Dwight said, "I'm visualizing every step of my approach, then lifting off and clearing the bar, landing in the pit." I said, "Do you ever picture yourself knocking that bar off with your elbow or foot?" Dwight said, "Never; why would you picture failure?"

That is what confident expectancy is all about. Having faith that success will come in your favor. Far too often, when we have a setback we continue to picture failure, rather than reprogramming our minds toward success. It is a mindset.

Transitioning to the NFL and college football as we approach mid-season, the failure that a T.E.A.M. has endured can be overcome by starting with a positive mindset—confident expectancy. That, along with faith and a strong and proper work ethic, will lead you on a path of success.

 Will you believe in confident expectancy believing good things will come your way?

After further review …

"I'm good at what I do," a professional with whom I am working said to me recently. Did he say that from a high level of self-confidence or was he "bragging"—bordering on arrogance? I heard it in a mild, straightforward convincing manner.

Having been around many professional athletes, I have often observed this high level of confidence. I can recall refereeing Super Bowl XI (Oakland versus Minnesota) when, in the fourth quarter, Vikings' quarterback Fran Tarkenton threw a pass that was intercepted by Raiders' defensive back Willie Brown, who returned it 75 yards for a Raiders' touchdown. Final score: Raiders 32, Vikings 14. As "Tark" walked off the field, he said to me, I'll be back." Was Tarkenton bragging? I didn't think so then nor did I think that of the professional previously mentioned. While we may notice this high level of self-confidence in athletes, it is also vital in all walks of life.

Allow me to digress for a moment—confidence, i.e., a firm belief in one's abilities, has nothing to do with gender, age, or occupation. What is of concern is the public display of one's achievement that might be classified as "showing off," which is too often seen in our sports stars.

As an example, a defensive player who "sacks" the quarterback then proceeds to strut around, pounding his chest as the quarterback is lying on the ground. Or, perhaps, after scoring a touchdown, two players leap toward each other and "chest bump." Sure, be proud of your accomplishment, but that is what you are supposed to do.

Would doctors who perform a successful surgery "chest bump" each other in the operating room? Does a sales person, just after a successful sale, run into the street and pound his/her chest proclaiming success? There are lots of examples of professionals who display *quiet confidence*. If you are really good at what you do and consistently do it well, it's not bragging when you quietly proclaim, "I'm good at what I do."

By all means, celebrate a success, but when and how you do it doesn't need to be proclaimed with a "look-at-me" attitude. In sports or sales management, enjoy your success but with caution. Should a sports official who makes a "good call" triumphantly demonstrate that on the field/court? In officiating, we remind officials, "You're only as good as your next call," which should be practiced by all.

 Will you enjoy what you do with a professional attitude without going to excess?

After further review …

"If you just get everybody *caring* about it the same amount—really, if you get the players to care about it more than the coaches do, that's when you have something special, I think," said Seattle Seahawks' starting quarterback Matt Hasselbeck. The "it" Hasselbeck was talking about is the culture of winning, i.e., success, that first year head coach Pete Carroll brought to Seattle. Culture is Carroll's term.

Hasselbeck continued, "Why do you need to change the culture? The culture's not the issue here, winning—or lack of it—is." Question: Can a change in culture influence winning? If so, how important is it to success to a T*E*A*M or for that matter to any organization/company? Moreover, how do you do it, and what factors are needed?

Several years ago, I was part of a study that identified what makes up the culture of an organization. We called it "climate," not culture. The words are interchangeable, and so are the factors, as you will see here. We studied a variety of schools to determine what those factors are that could change the climate of a school from the negative to the positive. Isn't that what Carroll wanted to do in Seattle?

While I am not familiar with the specifics that Carroll used, I write with confidence that among them were similar elements we discovered in our climate research. We found these seven to be of vital importance in improving climate: one, humanness; two, opportunity for input; three, caring; four, individualization; five, supportiveness; six, innovativeness; and seven, suitability of working conditions. While you may want to add others, it is apparent that these seven can be deciding factors in businesses and corporations, as well as in your community and family, and, of course, on a T*E*A*M (Together Everyone Accomplishes More).

Carroll's Seahawks finished only seven and nine, but won the NFC West division, then defeated Super Bowl XIV champs the New Orleans Saints (41-36), before losing to the Chicago Bears (35-24). Carroll's culture, call it mindset if you wish, certainly included the aforementioned factors and will be vital to the 'Hawks' future.

So, what will Jim Harbaugh in his rookie year (2011) bring to the San Francisco 49ers to improve their culture and thus their performance? Of course, the same is true of other new head coaches in the NFL: John Fox (Broncos), Ron Rivera (Panthers), and Fred Shurmur (Browns).

 Will you create a positive climate/culture/mindset in your organization?

After further review …

As this is being written, our country—the good 'ol U.S. of A.—is experiencing a government shutdown. No, this TUNNEY SIDE is not jumping into that egregious political mess. Better we establish a mindset that helps us look forward to brighter days. But how? Perhaps we focus on what each of us can do to maintain a positive outlook. Since these writings center on sports, let's invest our interests there. Participating in what our favorite NFL, MLB, NHL, NBA, or college T*E*A*M may be doing can help keep us balanced. That's important during a national crisis.

"Change the way you look at things, and the things you look at change" is a theme I often use in presentations to corporate America as well as in my leadership training sessions. Many are fearful of change, yet we need to treat change as a friend with the attitude that only through change will growth occur. Note that not all change is growth, but change is vital for growth.

Change was the subject recently when talking with a couple of my grandkids (we have sixteen!). They asked me what sports I played when *I* was a kid. I responded: football, basketball, and baseball—since I also thought those were the names of the seasons of the year. Then they asked what fast foods I ate. I said, "We didn't have fast foods when I was growing up; all the food was *slow!*" They jumped up saying, "C'mon, Papa! Seriously, where did you eat?"

I said it was a place called "home." And Mom cooked every day! When Dad got home, we all sat down together at the dinner table, hands washed and hair combed. If I didn't like what Mom put on the plate, I was allowed to sit there until I did like it. I didn't have the heart to tell them about how I had to have permission to leave the table.

I completed the picture by telling them, "You see, in those days some parents never owned their own house, never set foot on a golf course, never traveled out of the USA, and never had a credit card or a cell phone. My parents never took me to games—I rode my bike. There was no phone in my room, since we only had one—in the hallway!" Yes, "The times they are a-changin'" (thanks Bob Dylan).

Will you not be fearful of change, but treat change as a friend?

After further review …

During a recent sports talk show, the interviewer questioned a Major League baseball manager why he didn't challenge a call on his base runner more vigorously. The umpire called the runner safe and another umpire on the field consulted with the one who made the call and (original) umpire changed his call from safe to out. The manager of the T*E*A*M for whom the call was reversed stormed out of the dugout to protest. As the manager began his tirade, the umpire said, "Coach, I blew the call." The manager was not concerned with the error by the umpire, but was upset that the call had been changed.

The manager's explanation was that in his many decades in baseball, he had never before seen that happen. More than that, however, is the attitude of the manager, after it was over. The manager said that his approach to calls that go against him and his T*E*A*M is that they're going to happen and, maybe, just maybe, a call or two will go his way on another day. He focuses on "just moving on."

Consider these two thoughts: one, should umpires on the same crew help each other on calls during the game? And two, should baseball include more use of the replay system (now used for home runs—fair or foul)? The NHL uses the replay system and officials do help each other on calls. The NFL has used the replay system since 1986 (26 years old this 2011 season) and officials do help each other.

This relates to our everyday living in that the manager's attitude is about "moving on." Once a decision has been made or a situation that happened is in the past, the question arises—what value comes from replaying it in your mind over and over? It's done—move on. The value lies in the future, not in the past.

As psychiatrist Dr. Viktor Frankl wrote in his book, *Man's Search for Meaning,* of the freedoms that may be taken away from you, no one can take away the freedom to choose what you want to think, to be, or to do. As we honor the fourth of July, let us celebrate that we have the freedom to choose.

 Will you choose to move on instead of weltering in the past?

After further review …

During the F.I.F.A. Women's World Cup 2011 soccer matches, the United States T*E*A*M defeated Brazil in the quarter finals, a sportswriter penned, "They (the U.S.) 'willed' themselves to victory." That U.S. team went on to defeat France in the semi-finals only to lose in an extra-time draw to Japan in the finals.

The penalty-kick shootout is a diabolic way to decide a champion. However, one must concede that sort of tie-breaker is one of the most dramatic finishes in sports. Others use "sudden death" or extra innings/periods or other forms of shootouts; no matter, the losing team often suffers an overwhelming sense of failure.

As a kid on the playground with darkness approaching, we used the "one-tie-all-tie" system of completing that day's game, since being late for dinner was not an option (at least in my home). That system doesn't work in today's game—we must have a winner—philosophy. Of course, when you have a winner, then you must also have a loser.

That being said, in no shape or form is our U.S. Women's Soccer team a loser. Goalkeeper Hope Solo, forwards Abby Wambach and Alex Morgan, as well as midfielders Carli Lloyd and Megan Rapinoe and the rest of the U.S. squad gave superior performances throughout the tournament. Japan, who had never beaten the Americans in 25 previous tries, was an awe-inspiring team. Japan's captain, Homare Sawa, who made that spectacular stab of a corner kick to tie the match at two-all, and has many friends on the U.S. team, said, "It was great to play such a good match together, in a sense."

While women's soccer has become more competitive than ever, the humility and respect the Japanese team displayed is a standard about what sports ought to be. Both teams are to be honored as champions for giving the world an attitude of courage, desire, and a never-say-die spirit. The NFL lays claim that on Super Bowl Sunday, the world stops. Well, this "super bowl" of women's soccer stopped the world (many who don't know an offsides from a header) to admire these champions. All Americans can be proud of the effort with the will of our young women and the glory they brought to the United States.

 Will you give your best effort no matter what the scoreboard shows?

After further review …

Occasionally, I'll talk with someone who always seems to have a complaint—"If I didn't have bad luck, I wouldn't have any luck at all." Words of encouragement don't seem to detour these folks; even explaining the Law of Attraction doesn't help. The "law" says you are what you think about or what you want to happen. It is more than just the power of positive thinking; it is planning and then acting upon your plan. The world of sports is full of this.

So, was it luck that Stanford University quarterback Andrew Luck didn't have when he wasn't awarded the 2011 Heisman trophy? Quarterback Luck was a season-long favorite to be selected as "the player deemed the most outstanding player in collegiate football." Was the lengthy publicity too much pressure or too much hype?

The 2011 Heisman was awarded to Robert Griffin III (better known as RG3) of the Baylor Bears (9 and 3). RG3's stats were exceptional. In post-Heisman interviews, Griffin was impressive in his character and personality. My concern with the Heisman trophy, but has nothing to do with Griffin, has always been that the awardees should be *seniors*, whose eligibility has been completed.

Griffin, a junior, is only the second "Griffin" to be awarded the Heisman—the first being Archie from Ohio State University, who received this award twice (in consecutive years—'74 and '75) and the sixth player from OSU. Luck, a graduating senior, would have been the second player from Stanford—the first being quarterback Jim Plunkett. In the NFL, Plunkett won two Super Bowls and was MVP in Super Bowl XV.

It is interesting to note that only about half of the Heisman awardees have been successful in the NFL, which says that being the most outstanding college player does not always translate to the professional ranks. This is where the "blessing" comes in—you don't have to be the best in college to move on. In fact, earlier on, you don't have to be the best at anything to later be successful.

Speaking of "blessings"—while there is never a wrong/poor time to count your blessings, this time of year reminds me what my father once said: "Count your blessings." The sharing of ideas in these columns is, indeed, a *blessing* for me.

 Will you "count your blessings" every day?

After further review …

Inattentional blindness? Huh? What's that, and what's it got to do with sports? Inattentional blindness is what magicians use to successfully perform their tricks of magics. It's as old as Houdini himself; I was going to say "as old as Giovanni Livera (the best magician/speaker I know," but Gio's not that old). Inattentional blindness diverts our attention elsewhere, even if our eyes never look away. Have you ever sat close enough and watched intently as magic was performed "right before your very eyes?" Your eyes never wavered, but you still couldn't figure out how the magician accomplished his feat. When I once asked Gio, "How'd you do that?" He responded, "Very well"—his pledge to secrecy.

Some may refer to magicians' tricks as "misdirection." Maybe so, but inattentional blindness is not the same. Misdirection causes you to look at a new subject. Inattentional blindness is a phenomenon that explains how one can fail to perceive what one is looking directly at. So, what's the sports connection?

This is my take on that replacement official's call in that MNF game between Green Bay and Seattle. Just prior to that "simultaneous catch," there was an obvious offensive pass interference committed by the Seattle receiver. Now, I'm certain that the official whose responsibility was to call that OPI foul knows what offensive pass interference is, and probably has called it many times. He was looking right at it, but didn't see it. Several thousand viewers saw it. So, why couldn't the official? Inattentional blindness. Eyes and attention were in two different places. By the way, had that OPI foul been called, the play and the game would have been over, along with any controversy about the winner.

A lingering question is how do we, in our daily lives, avoid inattentional blindness? For example, talking on one's cell phone—Bluetooth® or otherwise—while driving "is dangerous because it misdirects our attention so that we fail to register what is happening right before our eyes," says journalist Alex Stone. United focus—eyes, mind, and body—enables us to overcome the splintered perception that can lead to the kinds of mistakes we saw in the Green Bay/Seattle game. Incidentally, what distracted that official's attention—not his eyes—is yet to be known. In fact, he probably doesn't know.

 Will you direct your attention to the important things that are right in front of you?

December 3, 2012

After further review …

Thirty years ago, January 10, 1982 actually, it was my privilege to referee the NFC championship game at Candlestick Park between the Dallas Cowboys and the San Francisco 49ers. The Niners, under the direction of quarterback Joe Montana and the wisdom of head coach Bill Walsh, drove 89 yards in 13 plays late in the game to score on a pass from Montana to Dwight Clark.

"The catch" is now famous in Niner lore. Montana, scrambling out of the pocket and being chased by Ed "Too Tall" Jones, threw wildly into the end zone. Clark, breaking his route, ran in the direction of that pass and leaped—some say higher than he had ever been off the ground—to catch the pass. The Niners prevailed 28-27 and proceeded to their first Super Bowl (XVI).

Moving from one Super Bowl T*E*A*M to another, the New York Giants benefitted from another legendary catch when wide receiver Mario Manningham (now with San Francisco) snatched a long sideline pass from Eli Manning with less than four minutes remaining in Super Bowl XLVI to set up the Giants' game-winning drive.

There have been many spectacular catches in the NFL's rich history, but none may have had more impact than the one that will never appear in Martellus Bennett's stats. Existing the field after a recent Giants' victory over the Green Bay Packers, the 6'6", 265-pound Bennett (who had his best game with some physical blocking and three catches for 44 yards), made his *fourth* catch of that evening.

Bennett said, "I was handing my gloves to some kids leaning over the railing, when a middle-age man tried to take the gloves, but a kid grabbed the gloves and ducked." Bennett saw the kid's maneuver, which caused the man reaching over the kid to fall about 15 feet toward the ground. "So, I just caught him; it wasn't that big of a deal," said Bennett. After "the catch," both fell to the ground unhurt.

"I guess I saved his life," said Bennett, a certified lifeguard and a fan of superheroes, who likens himself to Marvel X-Men's Cyclops. "I've been 'catching' people for a long time. I was happy the guy was okay."

 Will you look for someone who might be falling and in need of a "catch?"

September 16, 2013

After further review …

Fourth quarter of the NFL's season opener between Denver and Baltimore: Broncos' second-year linebacker Danny Trevathan angles underneath Ravens' Ray Rice on a short out pattern, cleanly plucks Joe Flacco's pass at the 30, and scampers untouched into the end zone. A touchdown gives the Broncos an almost insurmountable lead, but Trevathan casually drops the ball just short of the goal line. The resulting "fumble" travels out of the end zone for a touchback and the Ravens are back in business on their own 20. Hey Danny! Ya gotta finish the play!

Questions abound: first and foremost, what was Trevathan *thinking*? Further, if you're his coach, what disciplinary action, if any, would you take? Trevathan's response to that first question was, "I thought I had crossed the goal line." Really? Not that Danny ever noticed, or measured, but NFL yard lines are four inches wide, while the goal line stretches to eight inches. Granted, the ball need only break the plane of the goal line's inside edge, but how much *attention* (key word) did he give to making sure he was fully in the end zone? The man-on-the-street's perception is that Trevathan was so excited about his interception and effortless touchdown that he began celebrating before the *fact* of the score. Ya gotta finish!

This raised the important question of how would you, as a coach (or teacher or parent) deal with disciplining your player/student/child? Would you take the "I-got-the-hammer-and-you're-the-nail approach"? This writer believes a better approach is helping the person to not repeat the offense. What thought could be instilled to help your young student/athlete remember to complete the task?

"Finish the job" is a usable mantra. Plant the seed that will help the other person grow. The following verse might also come in handy, when personal glory jeopardizes the team's success:

Sometime when you're feeling important,
Sometime when your ego's in bloom,
Sometime when you take it for granted
You're the best qualified in the room,
Sometime when you feel that your going
Would leave an unfillable hole,
Just follow this simple example
And see how it humbles your soul.
Take a bucket and fill it with water,
Put your hand in it up to the wrist,
Pull it out and the hold that's remaining
Is a measure of how you'll be missed.
Be proud of yourself, but remember, there's no indispensable person.

 Will you put "finish what you start" in your mindset?

After further review …

The legendary Frank Sinatra often said that Tony Bennett was at the top of his list as the greatest singer *ever*. No argument here. Anthony Dominick Benedetto sings a beautiful song titled "The Music Never Ends," written by Alan and Marilyn Bergman. Its theme is: How do we keep the music playing? It's a mantra for living. Tony, at 88, is still doing some 50 performances annually—a feat admired by many octogenarians, as well as those wanting to be octogenarians.

As I watched 64-year-old Diane Nyad walk out of the water on that Florida coast recently, I never asked why; only just "wow!" Nyad had failed in that same attempt—a swim from Cuba to Florida—four times previously. That 110-mile swim is something one doesn't take for granted. It is an inspiration to many; if a sexagenarian can be persistent and achieve her goal, so can we.

As one ages, the incentive and effort required to continue exercising tends to diminish. Many thought that my late friend, Jack LaLanne, was crazy to perform physically as he did; he would be 99 tomorrow, but left us at 96. His wife, Elaine, carries on his fitness mantra today. This writer is an admirer of the LaLanne's efforts and determination, as I am of Nyad's.

Keeping your body healthy with the anticipation of living a longer life sure seems like a good idea; yet, how do you keep the music playing, how do you make it last, how do you keep it from fading too fast? Physical exercise on a regular basis is a good plan. Does that mean every day? Not necessarily, but setting a self-imposed schedule, then keeping that commitment to oneself, would be a good start. But wait, "I don't have the time," you say. Time?

That's what an exercise plan can do for you, i.e., give you more *time*—as in longevity. Your spirit is the determining factor, as it was for Nyad and the LaLannes. As I learned long ago, it's *mens sana* in *corpore sano*. For great inspiration and better information, pick up my colleague Tara Rayburn's just released book, *100 Easy Healthy Habits*.

 Will you keep up your spirit so your body will do so as well?

2 CHARACTER

October 12, 2009

After further review …

"Cause I'm the hall monitor," said nine-year-old Lin Hao, the Chinese schoolboy who marched in the opening ceremonies of the 29th Olympic Games in Beijing with China's flag bearer, 7'6" Yao Ming. Yao Ming, of course, you know as the Houston Rockets' NBA star, who played in the Olympic games for his native country China.

Lin Hao, perhaps, is a name you don't know—yet. When an earthquake hit Chengdu's Sichuan Province, China, killing 70,000+ people, Lin Hao was among those buried beneath the rubble, yet survived. Lin Hao had pulled a classmate out of the rubble, and then ran back in to rescue another, when he was caught in the tumbling walls. Alive when the rescuers got to him, Lin Hao was asked "Why did you back into that building that was crumbling?" Here was nine-year-old Lin Hao's response: "Cause I'm the hall monitor." You may call it responsibility, or leadership, or determination. Whatever you call it, please put "hero" next to Lin Hao's name. Extraordinary!

There is no question that the spectacular opening of the 29th Olympic Games was the finest I have ever witnessed. The precision and splendor of that opening was exceeded only by the people who directed and performed in it. It was easy to be convinced that the light show, the drumming sequence, and especially the "cube" happening was controlled solely by electronics. I was delightfully surprised when it was not, as the performers beneath those cubes popped their heads up at the conclusion. Extraordinary!

Zhang Yimou, who directed the opening ceremonies, said, "We (meaning every "cube" performer) worked for four months—eight hours a day—and we never got it perfect—until that opening night performance." Personal responsibility and a "never-give-up" attitude, coupled with *teamwork*, gave the world China's extraordinary best.

Critics knocked the Chinese performers as "sterile" and lacking passion (they missed the fact that there are 1.3 billion Chinese). I disagree. When you witness perfection, it may appear "sterile" and "passionless," but what often is missed is the extraordinary effort given to achieve perfection. Extraordinary performances are given by ordinary people giving extra effort to perform the extraordinary.

 Will you practice responsibility when it comes your way?

After further review …

"By rights, the NFL should be able to celebrate a history of abiding enlightenment," writes Alexander Wolff in the October 12, 2009 issue of *Sports Illustrated*. The subjects of Wolff's article were Woody Strode (#27), Jackie Robinson (#28), and Kenny Washington (#13), who made up the backfield of the 1939 UCLA Bruins.

My father was Kenny Washington's high school coach (Lincoln–Los Angeles). I met Jackie Robinson when he was a halfback at Pasadena (California) Junior College. Other than Fritz Pollard, a black quarterback in the 1920s, Washington became the modern day (after WWII) "first" black NFL player.

Gridiron magazine called Washington "the greatest football player we have ever seen." Legend has it that Kenny once "threw the ball 100 yards." My dad said it was true—not legend. (Kenny says it was only 93 yards.) I stayed close to Kenny in his later years (he died at age 52), since he had been part of my father's *character* and *courage*. My dad's character was to acknowledge Kenny's athleticism, not his skin color, and the courage to support and encourage (there's that word courage again) him to go to UCLA and on to the NFL. Few NFL teams had black players; others (George Preston Marshall, Washington Redskins owner, as well as George Halas, owner/coach of the Chicago Bears) chose to keep their teams "lily-white," as Wolff says in his article.

The NFL didn't move much beyond the segregation that blacks faced in the 40s, 50s, and into the 60s. Doug Williams, a black quarterback, led the Redskins (yes those same Redskins) to a Super Bowl title in 1988. Today's black players are not only dominant in the NFL, but respected as well—except for those few who tend to imperil the game by showboating and trash talking.

While the efforts of the NFLPA are working toward benefits for current and retired NFL players, we must not overlook, but applaud, the ongoing DIRE Need Fund and the Caring for Kids program of the NFLA (alumni). Under the 17-year tenure and leadership of CEO Frank Krauser, the character and courage that the NFLA promotes stands tall, along with those who supported and encouraged the Washingtons, Robinsons, and Strodes some 70 years ago.

Much has yet to be accomplished in helping indigent former players (of all colors). Only when the NFLPA and the work of the current NFLA come together, along with a better effort from the owners, will character and courage win out.

 Will you keep character and courage first and foremost in helping others?

After further review …

"Play the hand you're dealt," may refer more to life than to a card game. The "game" of life may deal you setbacks and unexpected challenges (often unwanted). The age-old expression "it's not what happens to you, but what you do about it that counts" has been used by many, but no more so than my speaking colleague W. Mitchell (visit www.wmitchell.com for more information).

Play the hand you're dealt certainly came into play (excuse the pun) at the 2010 U.S. Open at Pebble Beach this month. The U.S.G.A., as well as many golf experts, predicted that shooting par would/could be a winning score. Par for those four rounds of the 2010 Open was 284 and that's exactly what the winner Graeme McDowell, from Northern Ireland, shot. Of the 83 qualifiers, each playing four rounds (332 rounds), only 32 golfers broke par (.09 percent) and only two did it twice during the tournament.

Those 83 golfers are some of the best golfers in the world, and their scores are often less than par in most PGA tournaments. We regularly see scores of 64, 65, and 66 for a single round with total tournament scores in the 260s. Were these professional golfers surprised that low scores would not be possible at Pebble Beach? Not at all, but some did expect to do better. Did they complain about the "conditions" that the U.S.G.A. established for the 2010 Open?

Well, the word "awful" was used by at least two golfers in post-round press conferences. I will avoid the names of those golfers since the purpose here is not identification, but substance. One golfer, when asked by the press "how it went today" said, "I played awful" (on a day that he shot 75—four over par). He was blaming himself for a poor performance. The second golfer, who shot a 74 on the same day, replied to that same question that, "The course conditions were awful."

The first played the hand he was dealt, while the second wanted a different hand. My point is obvious: All 83 golfers were dealt the same hand. Yes, the course played tough—tougher than most. Seldom, if almost never, can you come out ahead if you blame others, the conditions, or the bad breaks that happen. It's best to look inward when things don't fall your way.

 Will you take responsibility for your performance or blame others when things don't go your way?

September 27, 2010

After further review …

The question is often asked, "Where do you get your stories/material for your Tunney Side of Sports articles?" Johnny Carson used to answer that question by saying, "As long as Ronald Reagan is President, I will always have material." I feel the same way about sports. The 2010 NFL season continues to provide material; how about this one:

Fairness versus loyalty. In week two, the Washington Redskins (1-0) played the Houston Texans (1-0) in Reliant Stadium. The game was close throughout and with time about to expire, the Redskins sent kicker Graham Gano in to kick a (52 yards) field goal for the win. One second before the ball was snapped, Texans' coach Gary Kubiak quickly called time out to "freeze" the kicker (a method others have used). The ball was snapped and the kick went through for the win.

But wait—the line judge signaled time out just before the snap, nullifying that successful field goal. After the time out, the Redskins' field goal team lined up to kick it again. That kick was wide right. The game remained tied and went into overtime. The Texans won the coin toss and marched to within field goal range. Kubiak sent in the Texans' field goal team. Neil Rackers, the Texans' kicker, lines up to kick what would be the winning points. Did Redskins' coach Mike Shanahan call time out just before the snap?

No, coach Shanahan did the *proper* thing and let the play continue. Rackers' field goal was "good." Houston won 30-27. This procedure, while legal, needs to be changed.

Interesting that quarterback Kubiak was drafted out of Texas A&M in 1983 by Shanahan, then the Denver Broncos' head coach. Kubiak played behind John Elway for nine years, and then was named the Broncos' offensive coordinator for 11 years—all under the guidance of Shanahan. It was Shanahan's support and recommendation that helped Kubiak be selected as the Texans' head coach in 2006.

Curious that Kubiak did not learn the character trait that his teacher applied. It is the hope and suggestion here that the NFL Competition Committee eliminates this procedure to take these kinds of decisions out of a coach's hands.

 Will you look at fairness in playing to win?

After further review ...

As a sports fan, are you getting all the sports info and opinions you need? Is it overkill? The "talking heads," as they are often called, are at it 24/7. The NFL has a cadre of experts on CBS, NBC, FOX, and ESPN, as well as the NFL network. Couple that with the NBA 2010 just starting (more panels); the NHL in full swing have their own experts; and now as we finalize the MBL with the World Series on FOX, et al, we hear a constant babble from these networks.

This is not to diminish the talent who appear on those shows. However, if you have trouble sleeping at night, those "panels are there for you—24/7. I recall some three decades ago when the idea of ESPN came about—what? A sports station 24 hours a day? Never work. Well, it has. Its success has spurred competition among the networks to meet the challenge and has captured viewers.

These TV channels—as well as radio and its plethora of talk shows—are seemingly what fans want. Views are hooked on "breaking news." Comments vary from game strategies to who will win the next game, followed by which pitcher the manager should use or which quarterback the coach should start or bench. Everyone has an opinion that seems to grab the fans' attention.

Today's talk shows go behind the field/court to opinions on the personalities and good/bad behavior displayed by players and coaches. Fans seem to thrive on the "bad behavior" scene.

Which brings me to my friend Tony Dungy, whom I've known since he played for the Pittsburgh Steelers after graduating from the University of Minnesota. Tony has been saddled with the title "hard path of righteousness." Seen regularly on NBC Sports, Dungy gives his honest opinion about which T.E.A.M. should win and/or which quarterback he would start.

However, when Dungy is asked about errant behavior of a sports star, or what punishment one should receive, his opinion is always about "doing what's right." Some viewers have criticized that. In fact, a Google™ search of Dungy's name with the term "holier than thou" yielded 871 hits one week. One search labeled him "an insufferable (expletive)." Tony doesn't force these comments on others; he responds to questions he is asked. He is passionate about his beliefs and doesn't hide them. He is not preaching, just being himself. That's refreshing in today's "talking heads" era.

 Will you give your honest opinion, whether politically correct or not?

December 27, 2010

After further review …

Was $25,000 enough? Sal Alosi, the NFL's New York Jets strength coach, made an ethical mistake during the Jets' loss to the Miami Dolphins in the 14th week of the 2010 NFL season. Alosi, standing on the sidelines, used his knee to trip Dolphins' punt cover-return player Nolan Carroll, who was running out of bounds (legally) to defend a punt return.

Unfortunately, that tripping by Alosi was not seen by officials. If it were, Alosi should have been "ejected"—meaning he would have to leave the field for the balance of the game. The NFL office officiating staff reviews "caught in the act" violations and assessed Alosi 25 large ones. Further, Alosi was suspended by the Jets for the remainder of the season—without pay—which has now moved to an indefinite suspension. Alosi has stepped up to admit his error and has taken full responsibility for his actions saying, "he wasn't thinking and is embarrassed for himself, his coaching staff, and owner." Thank you, but…

What about players who intentionally "hold" an opponent during a play? Or intentionally grab the facemask of an opponent? Or knowingly commit a foul in any sport? Are these ethical-type decisions or merely acts that are committed in the heat of the battle? Is there a difference? Certainly, is it not fair to put an ethical decision of this type in the same category as Enron, WorldCom, and Madoff indiscretions? Are ethics measured on a 1 to 10 scale?

The point is, of course, "just do the right thing." Do we really need officials in sporting events? Or police on the streets? Or armed forces to keep us from evil-doers? Indeed, there are evil-doers among us. Can ethics be classified like that old saw that says: "No such thing as being just a *little bit* pregnant?" Certainly, there are degrees of evil, e.g., murder, cheating people out of their money, etc. While not in the "crime" category, tripping an opponent as Alosi did is an "unsportsmanlike conduct foul" and punished as such.

We all may do "unthinkable" acts. But most of them are not on national TV. It is the belief here that Coach Alosi is a good person whose mistake may help us remember to "think before we act." Let's move on.

 Will you live an ethical life in everything you do?

After further review …

Enjoying the game of golf has been part of my life for the last three decades. Living on the California coast, we get to play most of the 365 days. This year was especially fun for everyone at the PGA tour/AT&T Pro-Am in Pebble Beach, as it was played in gorgeous, shirt-sleeve weather.

While watching those professional golfers and their amateur partners, my attention was drawn not only to the etiquette of all the players, but the observance of the rules of golf. Golfers, like most athletes, are fierce competitors. When golfers achieve a par on a hole, they wonder why they didn't make a birdie or "shooting" 74, wonder why they didn't get 73—ferociousness at its best.

Having spent much of my adult life as an official in football and basketball, the proper enforcement of rules is always important to me. Golfers, for the most part, call violations on themselves. Moving a ball illegally, even though inadvertently, is a rule violation and must be called. Occasionally, an opponent will call such a violation to the attention of the other, but without anger or bitterness found in other sports.

What is interesting in today's electronic age is that golfers sitting at home watching on television may catch a rules violation having been overlooked by the golfer and immediately text or phone to those in charge, pointing out said violation. Those in charge then may assess the appropriate penalty even to the point of DQ. I am not in favor of this. Other sports don't allow it.

In the NFL, NBA, and NHL, there is, of course, a review of fouls and violations. These reviews are conducted by experienced supervisors, not by fans. In the NFL, one network employed a former official to sit in the booth (or studio) and rule on fouls and violations, but without changing the call. It would be chaotic if fans were able to call in during a game and identify a foul or violation that was not called on the field. Even the Madden '11 video game doesn't allow this.

Think about your job as a parent or teacher or sales person or CEO, etc—what if a camera followed you around and recorded your every move/action or inaction?

 Will you play by the rules even when no one is watching?
(Note: The aforementioned is the definition of character.)

April 4, 2011

After further review …

They tell the story about the college football player who was late to practice. After putting on his gear, he walked past the head coach who questioned the player why he was late. "Sorry, coach," the player replied, "but I was in the library finishing a paper that was due tomorrow." "The library?" questioned the coach, "you're a football player for this university; don't spend my time in the library." The hot topic today is—should college athletes be paid?

The question of student-athlete lingers: is a player an athlete first and a student second or vice versa? The time demands placed on college athletes today are considered by many as extreme, if not unreasonable. Even at the high school level, young players are often required to attend workouts/weight lifting programs in the very early morning before attending their first class.

With NCAA coaches' salaries in the multi-millions, many often making far more than their college presidents, have we lost the purpose of a college education or should we change our thinking to go along with today's attitude? Since vast amounts of money are being poured into colleges for salaries, equipment, and facilities, should the players get some of that? If so, how is it to be divided? Would starters get more than reserves? Would a quarterback get more than a woman swimmer? Since much of this money comes from outside gifts and donations, who decides how the money is to be divided?

With money as the issue, college players who have NFL talent must complete three seasons/years before being eligible for the NFL draft. Do those players even to go class after their season is over in December? In the NBA, a high school player with that talent must wait until he is 19 or attend a college for one year before being eligible. MBL and NHL have no such restrictions on eligibility.

The late and legendary college basketball coach, John Wooden is quoted as saying, "When you come on the basketball floor each afternoon, for the next approximately two hours, you are a basketball player. That is all. As soon as practice is over, you are not a basketball player. You are a student at UCLA."

 Will you look at Wooden's statement as realistic or unrealistic in today's athletic programs?

After further review …

As the fall sports' season progresses, have you noticed that "in order to win," a T*E*A*M (Together Everyone Accomplishes More)—players and/or coaches—often feel it necessary to develop a hatred for their opponents. Animosity has no place in sports. Intensity is essential; however, it is important that we don't get those two mixed up.

Coaches, in getting their teams "psyched-up" for a game, have used hate as a tool to build intensity, often in the guise of T*E*A*M spirit. Wrong. T*E*A*M spirit is vital toward success as it builds camaraderie, which is not only important in sports, but serves us well throughout life. "I've got your back" is a phrase often used to build teamwork.

The value of sports can be life-long. Those values need to be remembered and are transferable to whatever people do in their life's endeavors. The family structure provides a relevant example when those in the family work together for the common good. Helping each other, especially in stressful situations is, indeed, the focus of teamwork. "Pick someone up" serves not only the person in need, but also gives the picker-upper a boost in energy.

Teamwork, on or off the field, replaces one's attempt to be self-important and puts EGO in its proper perspective. Steve young, the NFL Hall of Famer and former quarterback of the San Francisco 49ers, said, "If you play alone, you'll be alone." The emphasis here is that while your individual effort is necessary for a team's success, you can't do it alone. When you strive for that goal, your attention is focused on your team's efforts, not animosity toward the opponent. Hating your opponent loses not only your basic intention, but diminishes the real reason you play the game. This prayerful poem may say it all:

Dear Lord,

In the battle that goes on through life, I ask only for a field that is fair.
A chance that is equal to all in the strife, the courage to strive, and to dare.
And if I should win, let it be by the code with my faith and my honor held high.
But if I should lose—let me stand by the road and cheer as the winners go by.

Will you keep your focus on your values and eliminate hatred?

After further review …

"Inquiring minds want to know …" is an expression that describes those who want to delve into what's-behind-it-all. An incident took place at Ford Field in Detroit recently that perked the interest of some, when the San Francisco 49ers defeated the Detroit Lions. Following the final gun/whistle, the winning 49ers head coach Jim Harbaugh jubilantly raced across the field, with his feet barely touching the turf, to give Lions' head coach Jim Schwartz the customary handshake. Harbaugh's handshake was more enthusiastic than perfunctory. Schwartz proceeded to chase after Harbaugh with not-too-nice words being exchanged between them. What happened?

Does it matter? Well, it seems so to those "inquiring minds." Why is the focus on that confrontation? Should the polestar be on why/how the 49ers won or why/how the Lions lost? Well, for one thing, this type of behavior on the part of coaches doesn't—or shouldn't—happen at the professional level (operative word being professional). Many watching that fiasco want to know who is at fault. Of course, if you are a Lions fan, the fault lies with Harbaugh and vice versa. Okay, what happens next?

Several remedies come to mind. Perhaps coaches, who always visit *before* the game, end up shaking hands and wishing each other well, should just give a friendly wave (not a "gesture") to the other after the game and head to their respective locker rooms. Further, as new stadiums are built, the egresses need to be at opposite ends of the field. Some have done so already, but that doesn't happen to be the case at Ford Field. And, finally, with both coaches stressing that insipid behavior will not happen again, NFL HQ took no disciplinary action against either coach.

What about sportsmanship? Is it too much for one to apologize when another is offended? It seems here that the *bigger* man is the one who steps up to offer an apology. Whether demanded or not, it only raises the stature of the man. Both of these coaches are energetic, enthusiastic, fired-up leaders of their teams, which invigorates their staff and players. That's a good thing. When their behavior turns to disrespect, that's a bad thing. As Billy Shakespeare pointed out, "Much Ado About Nothing." Let's move on.

 Will you display proper behavior in issues of confrontation?

After further review …

"C'mon man!" is a favorite expression created by an ESPN crew on its Game Day program. This ESPN T*E*A*M of football experts shows slips from games wherein players "mess up." For example, should a pass hit a receiver in the facemask after going right through his hands, one of the announcers exclaims, "C'mon man!"—meaning that was an easy catch for an NFL player to make, but he messed up; or a quarterback who flubs a snap from the center or a running back who fumbles the ball without anyone near him—then you will hear, "C'mon man!"

This expression brings to mind Buffalo Bills' wide receiver Stevie Smith, when after catching a touchdown pass to put the Bills ahead 14-7, celebrated by making fun of New York Jets' wide receiver Plaxico Burress, who had spent 20 months in prison after shooting himself in the leg in a nightclub with an unlicensed gun. Smith imitated that incident as he pranced around the end zone for which he was penalized 15 yards (unsportsmanlike conduct). The Bills then had to kick off from their 20-yard line, giving the Jets great field position. Four plays later, the Jets tied the score with a pass to (you guessed it) Burress. "C'mon man!" The Jets won 28-24 and Smith was fined $10K by the NFL.

On Thanksgiving Day in front of a nationwide audience, Detroit Lions DT Ndamukong Suh demonstrated his ugliness by stomping his foot on Green Bay Packers' guard Evan Dietrich-Smith's arm. Dietrich-Smith had blocked Suh, and while entangled on the ground, Suh shoved Dietrich-Smith's head into the turf two to three times, then proceeded to get up and stomp on Dietrich-Smith's arm. Suh was ejected from the game, and the Lions were penalized 15 yards. The next week, the NFL suspended Suh for two games, without pay of course, costing him $165K+ in salary. Suh had already been fined by the league $42,500 this season for flagrant hits on the quarterbacks. "C'mon man!"

So what is it that seems to transform good—even great—sports stars into nincompoops on the field? Athletic competition, especially by professionals, needs to be one of respect. As my father once told me, "Always act like a gentleman toward others, not because they are, but because you are."

 Will you respect others even in the face of contentiousness?

After further review …

"The trouble with putting people on a pedestal," someone once told me, "is there's not much room to move around." And people like to have room to move around. Webster defines "to put on a pedestal" as "to glorify; idealize." Most of those elevated to pedestal status are not seeking adulation, but accept it with humility. Please understand; granting an honor or recognizing one's achievement is perfectly acceptable.

Unfortunately, we have seen too many leaders who have ascended to the top, then forgot that what got them there was their T*E*A*M. Leading by recognizing others is an essential part of leadership. Some who become leaders become powerful, and then sit atop that pedestal and shut others out. Most become leaders because of what they know, and too often forget the art of listening. It may be that they don't forget to listen, but choose not to for self-serving ends. It's a paradox of power.

This may have been the case with former and now deceased Penn State football coach Joe Paterno, whom I admired for many decades. It's common in corporate America as well. The HBO film "Too Big to Fail" provides such an example. In Paterno's case, it is obvious he overestimated the importance of his renowned football program compared to the child protection issues taking place around him. JoePa's statement of "I should have done more" came too late.

A different figure dropped from his pedestal in Columbus, Ohio, when Ohio State University's football coach Jim Tressel, aware of misconduct on the part of his players, put winning ahead of integrity. He was fired, as was Paterno. But OSU president E. Gordon Gee tried to resurrect Tressel on that pedestal when he said, "I'm just hopeful the coach doesn't fire me." President Gee then resigned.

When college football coaches' salaries far exceed those of college presidents, which we find on many campuses today, we have lost the value of our higher educational system. The funds generated by football do support many programs and services that would otherwise go vacant. Yet, when those in charge overshadow the real essence of their educational institutions with their power, often called executive bullying, someone has to step up. The NCAA did.

 Will you treat your leadership position as a privilege, not a right?

After further review …

USA Today recently ran an article about whom viewers *trust* as sports broadcasters. The story was not to criticize the personalities, but to ask the reader if the broadcaster was truthful or was it just hype. Having known sports broadcasters for over a half century, the conclusion here is that every one of them wants to be honest, yet free speech is not always a privilege. So, do you believe sports broadcasters or do you think some say what the networks dictate?

On the playing field, trust is a vital factor. Examples are plentiful: the quarterback trusts that the receiver will run the play that was designed, practiced, and ordered. If the receiver does his job, can he trust the quarterback to deliver the ball as planned? Examples are present in every sport, especially even in real-life situations.

Trust is huge in personal relationships. Trust must be there for relationships to succeed. Do you trust the people/companies you do business with? If you don't, that relationship will probably cease to exist. Trust is simpler than you might imagine. "If it's to be, it's up to me" is a mantra to live by; in other words, do you keep the promises you make? Moreover, do you keep the promises you make to yourself? If you can do that, keeping promises to others is easy.

Being truthful is a habit; but so is lying or making excuses. "Don't be an alibi-like," my dad used to tell me. In other words, don't make excuses, but *own up* to an issue. It's called accountability. Others will trust and respect you if they believe they can count on you. All too often, when we make a mistake, the first words out of our mouths are those of trying to cover it up.

Transparency is a key element in being trustworthy. How often do we see government, corporations, or universities trying to cover up their mistakes or misdeeds? Does the word *integrity* come to mind? Transparency is the password in the profession of sports officiating. Television replays, albeit with their faults, allow the viewers to see what happened. The game official is more vulnerable than ever. Building trust is a constant effort.

 Will you be honest with everyone, every time, in order to keep trust first and foremost?

After further review …

Lance Armstrong's recent interview with Oprah Winfrey on OWN (the Oprah Winfrey Network) was to be an admission by Armstrong of his performance-enhancing drug (PED) use. Was it? "It was pretty forthcoming, but he did not come clean in the manner expected," said Winfrey following the 2.5 hour session. Was Oprah expecting too much?

Armstrong's choice of the Winfrey show to "admit" his use of PEDs was as self-serving as LeBron James announcing at a 2010 media event staged on ESPN that he was taking his talents to South Beach. Much different in content and magnitude, of course, but why wouldn't James just make the switch without the bombast? And why didn't Armstrong simply "come clean" to the U.S. Anti-Doping Agency (USADA) or the International Racing Association?

While the use of PEDs, in any sport, is cheating, Armstrong's incessant, arrogant denials and the way he bullied fellow cyclists, their wives, and the media constituted his strategy of attacking the truth-seekers to preserve his virtuous reputation. Armstrong cheated himself, his sport, and all those who found inspiration in his battle against testicular cancer, including many who work so endlessly for his *Livestrong* Foundation (www.livestrong.org). How do we best communicate, especially to kids, the value of being truthful and the damage done by cheating?

In the summer following my sixteenth birthday, I was granted use of the family car to go on a date with my father's strong admonition to "be home by 11:00 p.m." I knew what he meant. Time seemed to speed up that evening, and as I rolled into our driveway with the motor off just before midnight, I knew I was in trouble. Tiptoeing across our kitchen floor, I heard the San Gabriel Mission bells chiming—bong (10), bong (11), and bong (12). Dad was sound asleep and snoring as loud as the bells, but Mom called out, "Jimmy, is that you?" "Yeah, Ma, it is," I replied with my heart in my throat. "Was that the mission bell chiming 12?" she asked from her back bedroom. Swallowing hard, I said, "Yeah, Ma, it was." I waited … and then she said, "Aw, go on to bed. Those bells haven't been on time for years." Whew! That lesson about being honest and earning trust has never left me.

 Will your truthfulness help you live the life you expect of yourself?

After further review …

Speaking to a diverse audience recently, I encouraged each to value teamwork in their families, in their workplace, and, by extension, everything they do. I remember so well what Hall-of-Famer Steve Young, former quarterback of the San Francisco 49ers, once said, "If you play alone, you'll be alone."

I describe teamwork by using the acronym T*E*A*M (Together Everyone Accomplishes More). If you take your hand and spread out your fingers, each of your fingers possesses the strength of a single digit. But if you clench them together into a fist, they become much more powerful. Muhammad Ali never won any fights with his fingers, but he sure did with his fists. The power of a T*E*A*M is discovered when everyone "clinches" together.

Loyalty to that T*E*A*M is what keeps it unified. Loyalty, a noun, is defined as "something to which one is bound by a pledge or duty." Google™ explains it as "a feeling or attitude of devoted attachment and affection." The teams I watched over the years of my career as an official met both these descriptions; but what is the source of that "devoted attachment?"

It's easy to cite several examples of pro athletes who play for their name on the back of their jersey, rather than the logo on their helmet. Loyalty, as with confidence, starts with reminding yourself to keep the commitments you make to yourself. If you can't do that, I believe you'll find it difficult to keep commitments you make to your T*E*A*M. No one wants to take away your individuality; it just means using your talents within the framework of your team. Teambuilding comes before teamwork.

Loyalty becomes visible when you are willing to admit your mistake, rather than alibiing your way out of it. Loyalty is strengthened when you step up to take responsibility for your actions. There is no better place to learn teamwork than in sports, or a club, or being in the band or choir. Loyalty learned in these venues will serve you well in your family, in school, in business, or in any area involving relationships.

The late Jim Murray, Pulitzer Prize-winning sportswriter, said it best when describing the qualities of a person he admired: "He makes the word loyalty a verb, not a noun."

 Will you make loyalty a verb in your everyday relationships?

3 COMPETENCE

iStock/Thinkstock

August 27, 2007

After further review …

Tiger Woods! Has there ever been a golfer who has dominated the tour more than this guy? Well, we were warned. Tiger first appeared on the Mike Douglas TV show at the age of four—more than a quarter century ago. Tiger's record in golf tournaments is second-to-none.

This is not to say we should overlook the achievements of Nicklaus, Palmer, Trevino, Miller, Venturi, Jones, or Hagen, to name a few "greats." But Tiger has raised the bar. Can his efforts be duplicated? Exceeded? Of course they can.

Let's look at a few characteristics that set him apart: 1) Talent—no doubt that his hand-eye coordination has to rank him in the 99th percentile; 2) His strength—changes in the way golfers exercise and train are at a new level with Tiger; and 3) Focus—Tiger's mental toughness would make NFL coaches proud. Mental toughness is defined as a combination of preparation and focus. The formula might be: P+F = Tiger.

After Tiger won his second consecutive PGA Championship at Southern Hills this year, a commentator mused: "Why doesn't someone challenge him?" I took that to mean the golfers in the rest of that field just laid down and let Tiger win. You kiddin' me? Stephen Ames was within one stroke of tying Tiger during that final round. Ernie Els cut Tiger's lead to one. Woody Austin was in the final pairing only to fall back. Every golfer in that tournament would have loved to beat Tiger. No one could—preparation and focus.

Sergio Garcia needs to be included in a group that wanted to beat Tiger. The problem with Sergio is that he didn't play on Sunday. Did he miss the "cut" after the first two rounds? No, he did play Saturday, but was disqualified. Missed his tee time? No—he signed an incorrect scorecard. He what?

Well, it seems that Boo Weekley in keeping Sergio's score (playing partners keep each others), recorded a 4 (par) on hole #17. Sergio actually "bogeyed" that hole for a 5. Was Boo at fault? Yes, but rule 6.6 a-d, page 28, says the competitor must attest to his proper score on each hole. Sergio lost his focus and was DQ'd.

With scores posted all over the course, how can this happen? Former CBS golf producer Frank Chirkinian invented the red number system (indicating a golfer was "under par") to help fans and golfers track how the golfer is doing. Maybe the PGA tour's new "ShotLine" system will solve this.

 Will you put preparation and focus first and foremost in everything you do?

September 13, 2010

32

After further review …

Michael Mauboussin, adjunct professor of finance at Columbia Business School, wrote in *Bottom Line/Personal*, Volume 31, "Don't trust your gut," subtitle "Why our first instincts are usually wrong." I agree, in part, about the "mistakes" people make in hasty financial decisions; I'm probably guilty as well.

My disagreement with "don't trust your gut" is from my 31-year NFL officiating career. Experience leads me to believe that an official's gut feeling in "making a call" (decision) in the heat of battle is usually correct. Let me explain.

Even with the advent of NFL instant replay, statistics indicate that the on-field official's call is in the neighborhood of being correct 94 to 96 percent of the time. Trouble is fans, players, and coaches want perfection, i.e., 100 percent accuracy—so do the officials.

Instant replay, first implemented in the NFL in 1986, is designed to correct erroneous calls. No official *intends* to make a bad call. An official is graded on every call, every no-call, in every game. Getting the call correct is not only a goal, but may determine playoff assignments.

"Trust your gut feeling" is based on several factors: one, an official's innate and learned abilities (let's call them skills); two, being in the correct position to make the call; and three, preparation—an official's continuous study and improvement in knowing the game.

There is another factor that is vital in making a call, and that is "anticipation." Despite one's training and preparation, the one element an official must guard against is making a decision before it happens.

Allow me to use, as an example, Jim Joyce, the MLB umpire who called the Cleveland Indians' Jason Donald "safe" at first base, preventing Detroit pitcher Armando Galarraga from a perfect game. Put yourself inside Joyce's head as he watched Donald race toward the base, as well as watching Galarraga cover the bag as the ball was fielded by the Tiger's first baseman, who is now throwing to Galarraga. Got it? All this action was racing through Joyce's mind, and Joyce, perhaps, is thinking what/who is going to get there first—the ball or the runner? Sometimes, the mind makes that decision before it actually happens.

The solution to that kind of mental exertion is wait…avoid anticipation. Let the play happen—then make the call. This advice can serve you well in many life situations as well.

 Will you let a situation develop and not anticipate what you "think" may happen?

After further review …

"Politely, I'm asking you to stop it. Just because you're frustrated, you need to stop what you're doing." Does that sound like a parent talking to a child? Or a teacher to a student? It certainly could be, but actually those words (reportedly) were the plea of Houston Texans' wide receiver #80, Andre Johnson, to Tennessee Titans' defensive back #31, Courtland Finnegan, during their game in Houston Reliant Stadium in week 12 of the NFL season.

You will recall that the Houston Oilers abandoned the city of Houston when Oilers' owner Bud Adams moved his franchise to Nashville to become the Tennessee Titans. Now, with both clubs being in the AFC south division, they play each other twice every season. Division rivalry can develop intensity and, for those loyal Houstonians who supported the Oilers when Bum Phillips was their coach, the intensity can bring on a heated rivalry.

Although most players on either of these current teams don't remember much of that era, fierce competition has developed between wide receiver Johnson and defensive back Finnegan. It just got to be too much in week 12, as the "pot" boiled over. Johnson grabbed the facemask of Finnegan just after the play started; then Finnegan grabbed Johnson's mask and pulled off his helmet. Then, the fisticuffs started with both swinging punches until officials and players broke it up. Both players were ejected from the game and fined $25,000 each by the NFL.

But no further suspension for either? Why not? As ugly as this was, the league has to compare it with all other fights and put it into a category—thus 25 large ones for each.

At the risk of taking sides (remember my book *Impartial Judgment*), Finnegan was voted by *Sports Illustrated* as the "sixth dirtiest NFL player." Perhaps Mr. Finnegan inherited fighting from his "Irish ancestry." Fighting is somewhat of an Irish tradition. My Irish grandfather could start a fight in a Christian Science reading room.

I've worked on the NFL field with some tough, hard-hitting players who prided themselves in their physical prowess, without being dirty. If I may ask, "Mr. Finnegan, why not strive to be the *greatest* player instead of the dirtiest?" To my knowledge, the (NFL) Pro Football Hall of Fame does *not* have a category for "the dirtiest player."

 Will you strive to be the best at what you do?

February 14, 2011

After further review …

Much has been written and talked about regarding the issue of Chicago Bears' quarterback Jay Cutler and "his decision" to take himself out of the NFC championship game with the Green Bay Packers. The Packers went on to win 21-14 and then, as you know, defeated the Pittsburgh Steelers in Super Bowl XLV, 31-25.

It appeared to viewers in that Packers-Bears game that at one point Cutler was "sacked" and came to the sideline limping—to the viewers, that sort of "limping" happens regularly in the NFL. The word over television was that Cutler took himself out of the game because of an injury to his knee, but no word of the extent of injury at that point. Cutler, then, was seen on the sidelines riding a stationary bike, used by players to keep loose. After a three-and-out to start the second quarter, backup quarterback Todd Collins replaced Cutler.

When word from the Fox sports announcers came that Cutler took himself out of the game, it gave many viewers the impression that, with such an important game at stake, maybe Cutler was "wimping out." It turns out that Cutler had a grade II torn MCL in his left knee and Bears coach Lovie Smith, along with their medical staff, decided not to risk further injury and/or that Cutler could not perform up to the standard expected of him. In post-season interviews, Coach Smith and the Bears players not only supported the decision not to reinsert Cutler, but gave strong support to his courage/toughness.

The real question being posed here is: Do players play with heart or with smart(s)? While these two are not mutually exclusive, which one, if given a choice, should—or will—govern? Players want to play and often play at *any* cost. One example is defensive end Jack Youngblood, who broke his fibula in the NFC championship game with the Dallas Cowboys, had it taped up and then played the entire Super Bowl XIV against the Pittsburgh Steelers with that broken bone. While this "style of play" is not suggested, it is more often the rule than the exception. It's difficult to keep players out of the game, no matter what injury they are experiencing. Thus, the NFL's policy insisting on medical approval in the case of concussions.

 Will you use your smarts in playing when your heart says "go for it"?

After further review …

"It's not the load that breaks you down—it's the way you carry it." As you read that statement, take a moment to reflect on the burden you may be carrying today. With the economic climate in our country and the constant concern about our involvement in war, along with the turmoil in leadership in so many countries, surely, this is a heavier "load" than we had wished.

Yes, I realize that these Tunney Side articles are intended to focus on issues in the world of sports and turning them into lessons that each of us can use for a better living, but stay with me, since that is where this theme is headed. Many of today's sports stars carry a heavy burden, more than we might imagine. This is in no way a defense of athletes who have fallen into disrepute; however, let me say there are those who carry their load very well.

The University of San Francisco Dons 1951 football T*E*A*M went 9 and 0, yet, was not invited to any bowl game—except one, which they turned down because they had two African American players—Ollie Matson and Burl Toler, who were not allowed to participate. Matson, who died last month at age 80, was so good that the (then Los Angeles) NFL Rams traded eight players to the (then Chicago) Cardinals for him. Toler never player in the NFL due to a leg injury in the college All-Star game, but went on to become the first African American official in the NFL. I was privileged to work on the same officiating crew with Burl for 11 seasons. Burl died in 2009 at age 81.

Game officials, as you well know, are called names, often not printable. Being the first black official, racial slurs (in the 60s) were often cast at him, not for his "calls," but personal epithets. When I would come to his defense, Burl would deny me the opportunity by saying, "They can't hurt me with those words." It was the way he carried that "load" that created the man he was. Burl's 25-year NFL career was marked by the way he carried himself both on and off the field.

By the way, the leading aforementioned quote is credited to Lena Horne, that sultry, sexy black singer who paved the way for black performers in Hollywood—"It's not easy being green."

 Will you carry your burden with strength and confidence?

After further review …

With the National Football League (NFL) and the NFL players (formerly called NFLPA—a union) still at loggerheads on how to split nine *billion* dollars, let's look at a new approach so that we *will* have a 2011 NFL season—and beyond. There are many concerns on each side that must be worked out. Here's an idea.

The owners want to make the NFL regular season 18 (now 16) games. The players say, "No way, too long." With four pre-season plus 16 regular-season games, plus the games played by those teams who qualify for the playoffs, the players are saying it's too much. During that type of season, the teams get one "bye" week. The players' reasoning is understandable, based on the fact that their bodies are unable to handle the physical abuse for that length of time.

Today's players are taller, stronger, weigh more, and overall have greater speed than ever before. It becomes more difficult to block a player who stands 6'8", weighs 290+ lbs., and has the speed to chase and often catch a speedy running back. Further, today's defensive backs are fairly equal in speed to wide receivers, yet bigger and stronger, as they create unusual force when they "launch" (missile-like) their bodies into opponents. The rule makers, aka the NFL competition committee, continue to scratch their heads to come up with rules for player safety, while trying not to change the game. With player safety being of paramount importance, how about this approach: one, have a pre-season of two games with a week off before the regular season starts, which would give the coaches a better chance to decide who to retain and who to release.

Second, start the regular season of 18 games after that bye week and play every weekend until the second week of November. At that point, have all teams take a two-week "bye" during which the players attend T*E*A*M meetings and workouts with the main purpose to "heal" their bodies. Third, start the balance of the season with the Thanksgiving games and continue with the rest of the season into the playoffs. That creates an 18-game season in the same timeframe as it has been with playoffs in January and the Super Bowl in February. While details and scheduling need to be adjusted to a given year, this approach has a chance to satisfy both parties.

 Will you look for ways to create solutions to an impasse?

After further review ...

It is often said, "Football is not a contact sport, it's a collision sport." "Ya gotta knock somebody down," coaches yell at their players. Today's players—high school, college, or pros—are bigger/stronger/faster with the word "collision" taking on a new emphasis. Further, with the expansion of the media (beyond TV), e.g., iPads® and iPhones®, today's professional players are more closely watched than ever.

Many of the coaches in our schools today come from a different background than the coaches of older generations. In the 1950s, 60s, and 70s, coaches were physical education and/or classroom teachers, where they saw their athletes as students as well as players. Today many—perhaps most—of our high school coaches are "walk-ons," coming from business and/or industry to coach today's athlete, after the school day is over. This is not to say that those with walk-on backgrounds are better or worse than the teacher/coach variety—just different in their backgrounds.

What is so strikingly different in today's world of sports is the hostility of the fans. Does this hostility come from those attending professional games where "win-at-all-costs" is the emphasis? Not only in the community from which this is written, but in many communities around our country (USA), the hostility toward coaches has exacerbated to the point of assault and battery toward all authority, with arrests and jail time for the attackers.

What's this all about, Alfie? No question that the increase of unemployment, loss of income, recession, and discontent with Washington D.C. and Wall St. has added unusual pressures to our adult world; yet, does it necessarily hold that their frustrations need to be transmitted to school games? Sports were designed, in the opinion here, to relieve those worldly pressures. That's why they are called G-A-M-E-S and not to be considered a matter of life and death. If you haven't observed parents attending Little League or school games, you will be (maybe not) surprised at the all-too-often hostile attitude displayed.

Part of being a T*E*A*M is learning to win graciously and lose with dignity. Losing is as much a part of learning about life as is success. As parents, we must be teachers modeling the expression "Excellence is good, exemplary is better."

 Will you lead by example, not just your words?

After further review …

"Worse day e-v-v-v-e-r," were the words one could read on the lips of San Diego Chargers' quarterback Phillip Rivers as he stood on his sideline, as the MNF game concluded. If you missed it, the Chargers were "charging" (sorry 'bout that) in the red zone with 48 seconds remaining at Arrowhead Stadium, and the score was knotted at 20-all in a tight division race with the Kansas City Chiefs. All Rivers had to do was to take snap, and then take a knee, which would have set up an easy field goal.

Rivers, arguably one of the best quarterbacks in the NFL today, had taken that snap from center Nick Hardwick literally thousands of times, not only in practice, but also in crucial game situations. This mishandled snap caused a fumble and was pounced on by the Chiefs' LB Andy Studebaker. The game went to OT, with the Chargers winning the toss, but then punting to the Chiefs, who went on to win 23-20.

How does this happen to a professional player, since that is what he does every day? Rivers was a *first* round draft pick in 2004 and has been the Chargers' starting quarterback in almost every game since. Well, these things do happen, even to the best. Recall that in game six of the recent MLB World series, the outstanding St. Louis Cardinals' third baseman David Freese dropped a routine pop-fly that most Little Leaguers could easily catch. Freese, ironically, ended up the WS/MVP.

This is not a rant against Rivers or Freese, but merely to highlight that mistakes do—and *will*—happen, even at the professional level. "Worse day ever"—hardly. When Minnesota Vikings' quarterback Tarkenton threw a costly interception in Super Bowl XI, he said as he left the field, "I'll be back." Bouncing back is just one of the many lessons one can take from sports, along with learning to work with others to achieve a common goal, as well as helping your teammate when a mistake occurs.

Sardonically, that MNF Chargers-Chiefs game was won by the Chiefs in overtime when kicker Ryan Succop, "Mr. Irrelevant"—the last choice in the 2009 NFL draft— kicked the winning field goal.

 Will you rebuild your confidence enough to "move on" after a blunder?

After further review …

You may recall your history lesson that the hot-headed D'Artagnan unites the Three Musketeers, who are down on their luck, in an effort to seize the French throne. If you substitute D'Artagnan with Harbaugh—John and/or Jim—and the French throne with the Lombardi trophy, you might get a glimpse of what these two were doing following the AFC and NFC championship game losses.

Can losing those two championship games create a chemistry that will bring the players of the Baltimore Ravens or the San Francisco 49ers closer together in their respective teams? The sadness of losing the AFC championship to the New England Patriots on the missed field goal by Raven's PK Billy Cundiff, a simple field goal he has made, perhaps hundreds of times, could be a strengthening element for them. Across the country, the fumble by Niners' rookie PR Kyle Williams that put the New York Giants in position to win in overtime, might just develop added strength and chemistry for San Francisco.

Should Cundiff or Williams solely be held responsible for the loss of their T*E*A*M? Absolutely not. If you believe in the mnemonic suggestion that T*E*A*M equals Together Everyone Accomplishes More, then you must agree that you win as a team and lose as a team—one for all and all for one. The unity created by those two teams certainly begins with their leaders, head coach John Harbaugh of the ravens and head coach Jim Harbaugh of the 49ers. A bit of irony you might say. Prior to the conference championships, there was speculation of a "Super 'baugh' Bowl"—for the first time in NFL history, brothers competing for the Lombardi trophy.

When one fails a test of a course, or misses a free throw while losing the event, that individual now faces dealing with failure. As teammates/friends rally around that person to offer encouragement, it brings out the chemistry needed to help individuals become a T*E*A*M. Legendary sportswriter Grantland Rice was spot-on when he wrote, "For when the one great scorer comes to mark against your name, he writes—not whether you won or lost, but how you played the game." All four teams in those two championship games played well enough to win—congratulations.

 Will you finish every event/contest knowing you did your best whether you won or lost?

After further review …

Linsanity has been a "breath-of-fresh-air" for New York City and the NBA. Linsanity is the nickname for New York Knicks (nickname/NY Knicks—get it?) point guard Jeremy Lin. Jeremy? How does the name Jeremy fit with Kobe, LeBron, Dirk, or Melo? Is he the first Jeremy in the NBA? Might be.

Gie-Ming, the 5'6" father of three, is the one responsible for naming his middle child Jeremy Shu-Hao Lin (correctly Lin Shu-Hao). Jeremy, now 6'3" and the 2012 NBA sensation, is a middle child. Aren't they the ones who suffer from middle-child syndrome? Psychologists say that the middle child often "fights harder for attention" and often gets "less praise than the other two." Maybe that's what inspired Jeremy to step up to be the scorekeeper for his older brother Josh's high school team. Now, at 23, he is the talk of the entire basketball world—the fans love him. Why?

Well, for starters, he is humble about his new found success, and, by the way, success is not so new to Lin. He was the captain of his Palo Alto High School (CA) basketball T*E*A*M that went 23 and 1 to capture the CIF Division II State Championship. When he sent resumes and DVDs trying to garner a college scholarship, he received zero response from Stanford, Cal, and San Jose State. Lin then walked on to attend Harvard.

Harvard? Yes, that Ivy League school not known for recruiting 6'3" Asian guys to play basketball. Lin not only made the Harvard T*E*A*M, but was twice All Ivy League (yawn). Undrafted by the NBA, Lin was invited to pre-draft workouts, eventually signed, but then cut by two teams—one his home town Warriors. The Knicks claimed him off waivers for about 1/20th of what Knicks' stalwarts Carmelo Anthony and Amar'e Stoudemire are making. At this writing, Lin ranks eighth in the NBA's PER (performance efficiency rating). Eighth!

Winning is only secondary to what Lin has meant to the NBA. His attitude, style, and demeanor are badly needed in that sport today. About Lin's "recent" star status, maybe Kobe said it best, "Players playing that well don't usually come out of nowhere, but if you can go back and take a look, his skill level was possibly there from the beginning. It probably just wasn't noticed."

 Will you look for those who might have a talent undetected?

After further review …

Several months after I refereed Super Bowl XI (January 9, 1977), I happened to meet up with Oakland Raiders' head coach John Madden. The Raiders had defeated the Minnesota Vikings in that Super Bowl 32-14. John was wearing the imposing Super Bowl XI ring given to him, along with the Raiders players and personnel, as a symbol of their victory.

I had known coach Madden both on and off the field for several years and felt comfortable kidding with him. So, I said, "John, that's a beautiful ring, but I don't understand. You and I were on that Rose Bowl field for the same three hours and 15 minutes, yet you received that beautiful ring, and the NFL gave me this Timex®. Why the difference?"

Coach Madden retorted, "Cause you don't care who wins." Wow! That's a startling, but very true, response. As an NFL official responsible for the precise operation of the game, who won was never important to me; officiating the game without prejudice was.

I recently read a newspaper article with the headline "NBA conspiracy theories: long shot or short lay-ups." The tenor of the story (I've seen several on the same topic) was that the National Basketball Association covertly controls which teams get to the finals by influencing the officiating. Ridiculous! I know many of its current officials and have known many over the years. Bashing the integrity of officiating is uncalled for.

Having officiated both football and basketball for over 40 years, it is apparent that officiating the game of basketball in today's style of play is incredibly difficult. With 7-foot, 250 lbs. players charging, blocking, dunking, and rebounding, it is often a contest more suited to the NFL field. How NBA officials determine who is responsible for the foul is beyond the casual observer's judgment. To suggest that the NBA attempts to subvert rule enforcement so that certain teams progress through to the finals carries the word "theory" all the way to "surrealism."

The days of "Donaghygate" are over. (Note: Tim Donaghy was a 13-year NBA official who served a jail sentence following his conviction on federal gambling and conspiracy charges.) Today's NBA officials have only one interest in mind: to call the game impartially using their best judgment. To suggest otherwise is farcical.

 Will you make your decisions based on your honest appraisal of the situation?

After further review …

"Heads up!" my dad used to call out, alerting me to such possible dangers as an errant pitch traveled toward my head when I was batting, or as a car approached as I was learning to drive. He must have blurted that phrase a thousand times. The message never failed. Being an admirer of my father, I adopted the same warning as a parent and coach, and whenever I could alert anyone of a possible risk.

While this expression is an ancient one, it certainly is popular today. The Centers for Disease Control and Prevention, with a primary mission of controlling infectious disease, has nonetheless joined the national discussion about sports-related head injuries. The CDC has an online training program, called "Heads Up," for coaches and athletes. NFL commissioner Roger Goodell has recognized the importance of such education.

Concussions are in the spotlight in the game of football. A recent report indicated more than 3,000 former NFL players, many well known, have filed concussion-related lawsuits. Tackle football played by secondary, college, and professional athletes is a physically violent game. Yet, with all the apparent risks of physical damage (e.g., concussions, broken bones, nerve degeneration), the majority of former players say they "would do it all over again." However, some of these same players have grave concerns about their sons playing football at those levels. Parents should also be "heads up" for their daughters and sons who play soccer—a popular sport with young athletes. The caution here is using "header" shots to redirect balls traveling 30 to 40 mph.

"Heads up" is also an expression used by former NFL Hall of Fame coach Don Shula, whose 347 victories gathered in a three-decade career will never be equaled. Shula always taught his players to block and tackle by "seeing what you hit." When you see what you hit, it requires keeping your head up. So many players in today's game, falsely protected by a plastic helmet and a cage facemask, believe leading with your helmet is a safe style of play. It's not!

And finally, former NFL coach Herm Edwards always told his players, when they were trailing in a game, to "keep your heads up." Edwards' instruction was for the benefit of maintaining poise and confidence.

 Will you be aware of potential rewards in keeping your head up?

After further review …

Seeking perfection is, indeed, a rightful purpose. The sports world not only *seeks* perfection, but *demands* "it." But, the "it" factor is puzzling. Mark Wiskup's book, *The 'It' Factor,* raises many questions as he attempts to answer that age-old question: What is "it"? How do you get "it"? How do you keep "it"? Wiskup subtitles his book: *Be the One People Like, Listen to, and Remember.* Sounds like something that would appeal to everyone. The author further states, "You're not born with 'it,' but 'it' can be acquired." Hmm…

Surely, you can name sports stars that seemed to have "it" in their DNA. You probably can also name others who seem to have "it," yet never performed to the level of expectations—theirs or yours. "Being the best you can be" is preached by coaches, teachers, and parents to the young, and yet, is perfection possible? You've heard it said, "You must always seek perfection; and while perfection may not be possible, *excellence* can be captured along the way." That expression may describe a way to reach "it."

Professional athletes are full time—that's all they do—wanting to perform at their best. However, we see mistakes happen at that level that are not expected. For example, in a recent MLB playoff game, a fly ball was dropped by a centerfielder whose level of fielding always had been exceptional. In another MLB playoff game, the umpire incorrectly ruled on an "infield fly" play. Both of them are full-time professionals, and both situations were costly errors. This is not to embarrass or castigate them, but to make the point that doing something full time does not ensure "it."

Recently, I was part of a television T*E*A*M producing a nationally televised event. The producer emphasized three points to his crew: one, overcommunicate; two, be where you're supposed to be and on time; and three, don't overlook the little things. In televising sports, where perfection is the goal, those three instructions may describe a path toward achieving "it."

Giving one's full, undivided attention to the task at hand (i.e., being completely focused) is vital in seeking perfection. Practice doesn't make perfect; perfect practice can be a way to achieve "it."

 Will you put forth your best effort in whatever you do to accomplish "it"?

4 COURAGE

iStock/Thinkstock

December 6, 2010

After further review …

I was encouraged to see the leadership stance taken by the NFL Tennessee Titans' head coach Jeff Fisher who removed Titans' quarterback Vince Young from the T.E.A.M. This decision by Fisher followed a verbal battle between the two, following their overtime loss to the Washington Redskins in week 11. While all of the "inside story" has not been revealed, it is the understanding here that Young used profane language—in a personal way—toward Fisher after that loss. What further irritated Fisher was that Young texted an apology rather than meeting face-to-face with Fisher. Ah, the younger generation and their technology. Fisher doesn't text.

Part of what is known is that Fisher was unhappy with Young's lack of commitment, work ethic, and effort. Reading between the lines, it would appear that the flare-up that happened after the loss to Washington was perhaps the "straw," etc. Many times, a strong disciplinary move by the leader (Coach Fisher) and the employee (quarterback Young) takes place after a number of "little things" have occurred.

Young was a first-round draft choice by the Titans in 2006 after an All-American career at the University of Texas. Fisher, who was a defensive back for the Chicago Bears, when they won Super Bowl XX, has been the Titans' head coach for 16 years—the longest tenured coach in the NFL today. The real story, for me, is "who's in charge here?"

Having observed the NFL for 50 years, I have noticed a "decline-of-authoritative power" in the NFL coaching ranks. The player-coach relationship has been broken with: one, money (players being paid—guaranteed exorbitant salaries and bonuses—much more than their "bosses"); and two, the heavy infusion of agents who negotiate the athlete's salary. Negotiations are conducted between the club's owner and the player's agent. The coach isn't involved.

I doubt we'll ever return to the Lombardi, Shula, Landry, Noll, Walsh era where the coach was "really" in charge. The authority of an NFL head coach must be absolute. The coach must be the leader "in charge." Absolute has to do with legal, ethical, and a sound philosophy of leadership practices. Hopefully, Titans' owner Bud Adams will support Coach Fisher in maintaining the role of the coach as its leader.

 Will you support a leader who leads with a sound understanding of his/her followers?

May 14, 2012

After further review …

The hype for the 30th Olympic Games, scheduled for London in August 2012, has already begun. The British have been working for many years to have a successful Olympiad, and certainly have a great model to follow in the 2008 games in Beijing. The Chinese set an almost unreachable standard with their excellent performance.

Thinking back to China and that summer, I am reminded of Lin Hao, perhaps a name that has slipped your mind over these last four years. His story bears repeating. Nine-year-old Lin lived in Sichuan Province's capital city of Chengdu when, in May 2008, an earthquake hit the area, killing in excess of 70,000 people. Lin was among those buried beneath the rubble, yet survived. Lin had pulled a classmate out of the rubble, and then ran back into the school building. The rescuers scolded him and asked, "Why did you go back into that building that was crumbling?"

"Cause I'm the hall monitor!" was the young boy's response. You may call that responsibility or leadership or determination, but whatever you call it, please put the word "hero" next to Lin Hao's name. It was that sort of personal responsibility and a never-give-up attitude that gave China high marks for excellence in the conduct of those Olympic Games. That never-give-up attitude was the theme of the address I was recently privileged to present to more than 400 down-on-their-luck men and women.

As we observe our young people today, many have that sense of "I'm the hall monitor" and exercise it without fanfare. The idea that every good deed warrants a parade down Main Street is a concept that needs correcting. As parents, teachers, and coaches, we need to encourage our young people to have the courage to step up without hesitation or expectation of reward to help others in need. Notice within that word encourage is the word "courage," meaning the ability to conquer fear.

Studying athletes, as I have done all my life, I find that the successful ones learn to manage fear, not avoid it. It takes courage to perform, whether it's in sports, music, dance, etc., and especially life. Those who have learned to manage fear progress through life with a greater sense of accomplishment.

 Will you have the courage to never give up?

After further review …

Westmont College, a small (1300+ students) Christian, liberal college, located in Montecito, California, won the 2012-13 NAIA Women's basketball championship. Not much of a big deal, most would say; happens to one of those small schools every year. Yeah, but ya gotta hear the "rest-of-the-story." A big thanks to my friend and colleague, *Los Angeles Times* esteemed sportswriter, Bill Plaschke, who recently wrote about this for the *Times*. It bears repeating.

Westmont's women's basketball head coach Kristen McKnight met Alex Moore, a Westmont kinesiology professor in 2003. Alex thought they were "made for each other," but Kristen didn't have time for romance—basketball was her passion. Alex was relentless. They married in 2008. On May 9, 2012, Alex underwent colon surgery for Crohn's disease, during which he tragically died due to a pulmonary embolism. Kristen was eight months pregnant with their first child. Seven weeks later, the baby was born. Kristen named her Alexis. Time for a sabbatical; I mean, come on, a grieving widow and a newborn; not Kristin—she barely took a day off.

Standing in front of her T*E*A*M in August, 2013 preparing for the season, she said, "I'm here and this is going to be a hard road, but I'm here." Kristin continued, "I'm going to be real; you're gonna see me cry a lot, but I have to do this." She didn't have to do it at all. Do courage, dedication, and commitment come to mind?

Winning 24 of 27 games for the Warriors to be the Golden State Athletic Conference champions, along with NAIA champs, would normally be the story; but it was actually the easy part. Members of the athletic department, the community, and dozen or so players all pitched in to take care of Alexis. Changing Alexis' diapers on an aluminum bleacher in the women's bathroom, and asking the men's T*E*A*M players to turn their heads (since both teams travel together on the bus), while Kristen breastfed Alexis, was just some of the many trials she endured.

Even Alex, then deceased, contributed. Two days after his death, while rummaging through Alex's office preparing for his memorial service, Kristen found these Bible verses on two Post-it® notes: "Encourage the oppressed, defend the cause of fatherless, plead the case of the widow;" and "Be strong and courageous and do the work, do not be afraid or discouraged for the Lord God, my God, is with you." Those were Alex's final words to Kristen.

 Will you use the strength of your courage to help you carry on?

5 FAMILY

December 3, 2007

After further review …

Parents love to take pride in their children, especially when their kids are doing well. Whether it be at home (chores), in school (studying, doing homework with their best effort), in their community (helping others), or on the athletic field (playing on a T*E*A*M). But what if you had a son (son for the sake of this story) who was a shining example of all of the above?

But wait—what if that were not one son—but two? And what if those sons not only excelled in college sports, but also, after graduating (key word: graduate) from college, went on to play professionally n the NFL? Both in the NFL? Yes, both.

Thomas Jones, who starred at University of Virginia, is a 5'10", 215 lb., running back for the New York Jets (#20), and the three-year older brother of Julius Jones, 5'10", 208 lb. running back for the Dallas Cowboys (#21). Wow! Would you be a proud mom and dad to sit in the stands and cheer for them?

But wait—what if they were playing in a game against each other? Who would you root for? Well, it was bittersweet for parents Betty and Thomas A. Jones (Big Thomas as he is called) as they sat in their seats at Texas Stadium on Thanksgiving to cheer for *both* their sons. Betty and Big Thomas, along with their family, all wore jerseys with "T. Jones #20" on one side and "J. Jones #21" on the other. Unbiased family loyalty stood out.

But wait—while the Jones boys continue to play this season and beyond, the "rest of the story" is really the highlight. Growing up in Big Stone Gap, VA (population 4,856), six traffic lights, a Huddle House restaurant that serves a $4.95 breakfast of eggs, hash browns, grits, toast, and bacon, the Jones boys, who also have six sisters, were the only two African American players in a predominately white school in an overwhelming white town. Race, at times, was a factor, particularly when the Jones boys played away from home. Big Thomas would remind his children, "It's not the color of the grocery bag, it's what's inside."

As kids, little Thomas and Julius spent their life in a basement with cracked flooring, wore patched jeans, and hand-me-downs, and, when pork chops were on the home dinner menu, had six pork chops for nine mouths. Church on Sundays required two trips, since only half could fit in the family car at one time. "Yes sir" and "yes ma'am" were paramount in their vocabulary. A strong family bond got the Jones kids through tough times.

 Will you take time to count your blessings?

July 5, 2010

After further review …

Today, July 5th, is the 45th anniversary of the death of my father, Jim Tunney, Sr. I celebrate this day every year because of the legacy he left. He was my role model and mentor. My dad was a teacher, coach, school administrator, and athletic official. He, along with my mother, now also deceased, "left the light on the others."

Pride is the one word that embodies the lessons my father left for me. I have often used *pride* as a mnemonic device (a reverse acronym if you will) to describe a path to follow. Pride in yourself, pride in your work, pride in your family. P*R*I*D*E: Personal power; Responsibility; Integrity; Determination; and Everyone.

P = personal power, not position power. You can engender goodwill among others by demonstrating your self confidence. Coaches can get more out of their players by lighting a fire in their belly, rather than kicking them in the butt. The haughtiness of position power—that is "look who I am"—often negates positive leadership.

R = responsibility means stepping up to make things happen. Too often, we wait for others to do the job. When you know that a task needs to be done, just do it—"git 'er done." If or when things don't work out, pointing a finger at others denies personal responsibility. When you do that, remember there are three fingers pointing back at you.

I = integrity. Just do the right thing. A sports official may make an incorrect call due to poor judgment, but if one's integrity is intact, stature will rise, not fall. Sports officials (or anyone in a position of authority) must hold themselves to a higher standard both on and off the field.

D = determination is a never-quit attitude. Players may lose their momentum, but, through determination, must never lose their confidence. Remember, when you do the right thing, good things will happen. "We must never, never, never give up," Sir Winston Churchill emphasized to his British subjects during the darkest days of World War II.

E = everyone, as in T.E.A.M.—Together Everyone Accomplishes More. Each of us needs all of us. Athletes, even those in individual sports, need others to help them achieve. You can't do it alone. As Hall of Fame quarterback Steve Young (San Francisco 49ers) told me, "If you play alone, you'll be alone."

 Will your legacy transmit value to others?

June 13, 2011

After further review …

Several Melrose High School players' faces currently portray their school colors—red! Melrose High, located in a Boston, Mass. suburb, has now become known infamously nationwide with bad news/good news. The bad news is that 11 Melrose varsity athletes have been suspended from competing in their school's athletic events for the next season (athletic competition for this school year has been completed). It seems that these young culprits were "caught" on Facebook® at an off-campus event in possession of alcohol and/or tobacco.

Social media certain has given new meaning to Melrose High's nickname of "Red Raiders." These 11 Red Raiders were seen "red"-handed with their pictures on Facebook. Young people have engaged in these kinds of "forbiddens" clear back to my high school days. As a former high school coach and principal, I have all-too-often dealt with these unfortunate incidents. In the past, however, the accusations were usually verbal, involving a long process of he-said/she-said denials. With their pictures now on Facebook, these offenses are difficult to defend.

For the "good news," the district superintendent said, "We're serious when we say athletics is a privilege, not a right." Wonder what part of "serious" these students didn't understand? The supe went on to say, "We are not trying to interfere with what happens outside of school, but if you're going to represent the school, we expect you to uphold that image 24/7. We understand that people make mistakes, but there are consequences."

Wow! Think we could get him to run some of our professional sports leagues with kind of commendable action? He is merely enforcing the commitment these athletes made when they signed on to comply with the MIAA (Mass. Interscholastic Athletic Association) rules. Every state association has such a requirement for athletic competition. Think we could get our sports pros to sign such a commitment?

How do we impress upon our youngsters that not only participation in sports is a privilege, but attending school to improve their skills with people who care about them is equally so? With the world being flat, our young people can readily see what better conditions for an education they have here compared to those in other countries. My hope is that the parents of these students will support the decision and not try to "protect" their kids by "getting them off." Accept it, learn from it, and move on.

 Will you be supportive of this disciplinary action?

After further review …

InSideOut Coaching is the title of a book by Joe Ehrmann subtitled, *How Sports Can Transform Lives.* Joe is a former NFL defensive lineman, drafted tenth in the first round of the 1973 draft by the Baltimore Colts. Ehrmann played 10 years in the NFL, after an All-American career at Syracuse University. In 1978, Joe was selected to play in the Pro Bowl, a distinct honor in those days. However, 1978 was the same year that his brother Bill lost his fight with cancer. Strange how things happen in our lives that have greater impact than honors we receive.

As a result, Ehrmann began to reassess his priorities, and spearheaded the construction of a Ronald McDonald House in Baltimore in memory of his brother. Joe then became an ordained minister, and today continues his ministry travelling throughout our country with a mission of transforming lives through sports.

With the unfortunate emphasis on winning at all costs confronting young athletes today, Joe's message is a breath of fresh air. His core philosophy is simple: build people from the inside out. Sure, you want to create winning teams, but not at the expense of damaging the person inside. When young athletes finish playing, what do they take with them to create successful lives off the field or court?

Former NFL coach Herm Edwards, a native of Central California and the subject of my book, *It's the Will, Not the Skill*, has, throughout his sports career, emphasized the value of playing the game to win, yet with the utmost integrity and high moral standards. Edwards played for the Philadelphia Eagles during the same era as Ehrmann, so he knows the kind of man Joe is.

TCMC (Transformational Coaches of Monterey County) has invited Ehrmann to be the guest speaker at an event to be held on May 2, 2012 at 7:00 p.m. in the CSUMB gymnasium. TCMC is a newly formed alliance of coaches, parents, and community members whose mission is supporting and inspiring adults to use the powerful platform of coaching to transform the lives of our youth. This evening event is free. However, funds are needed to support this important program. You can help with your donation to the Boys and Girls Club of Monterey County/TCMC—a 501c3.

 Will you be a part of helping our youth become the best people they can be?

After further review …

The United States Golf Association plans each year for the U.S. Open to be the purest test of golf. The 112ᵗʰ U.S. Open held on the Lake course at the San Francisco Olympic Club was, indeed, just that and, maybe (too much) more. Now, don't get ahead of me. The Olympic Club is a wonderful golf course. The layout itself is challenging, but did the USGA need to make it "that" tough? The champion was 28-year-old Webb Simpson, who was ranked 208th when the 2011 PGA tour began, but had a great year by finishing second on the money list, thereby moving him up to tenth.

He shot 68 on each of the last two rounds with the final round being on Father's Day. His wife, Dowd, expecting their second child in July, walked all four rounds (72 holes and 281 golf shots) with her champ. When Simpson finished, others were still on the course with both Jim Furyk and Graeme McDowell having a chance to best that 281. The Simpsons (no, not those TV guys) sat in the Olympic Club clubhouse and while waiting for Furyk and McDowell to finish, watched a video of their 16-month-old son, James, who was back home in Charlotte, NC, taking his first steps—a relaxing diversion.

From the 16ᵗʰ tee through the 18ᵗʰ green, Furyk and McDowell weren't up to the challenge. But what happened to the World Golf Ranking's number one player, Luke Donald? He missed the cut as did the number two player, Rory Mcilroy; and Phil Mickelson, an often Open runner-up, finished 65ᵗʰ—26 over par. Tiger, tanked 4ᵗʰ, finished 25ᵗʰ—seven over par. The 2012 Masters champion, Bubba Watson, missed the cut with the comment, "It (the course) beat me up." Does the U.S. Open course have to do that?

There are a lot of professional golfers on the tour now who seem to continue to outdo each other week after week. Of the top 11 ranked golfers, only Simpson, McDowell, and Jason Dufner finished in the top 10 at this U.S. Open. And what lies ahead now for Simpson? The British Open? Nope, Dowd is due to birth their second child about that time, so Webb will be staying home. Looks like golf finished a distant second to this family.

 Will you treat your family with a #1 priority?

6 HONOR

After further review …

On My Honor, I Will is a wonderful book just released by my friend and colleague Randy Pennington. The subtitle is *The Journey to Integrity-Driven® Leadership*. It makes a wonderful present for those involved in leadership, as well as anyone who has a responsibility to and/or for others, e.g., coaches, teachers, parents.

The title reminds me first and foremost of the Boy Scout oath that I said often as a scout (Troop #9, Alhambra, California). At that young age, perhaps we really never knew how significant that oath would mean to us later in life. We faithfully recited it, and, of course, intended to practice it as Scouts, but the real value may not have sunk in then.

Unfortunately, former NBA referee Tim Donaghy never was a Boy Scout and never learned this oath; or if he did, it got lost somewhere in his adult life. Donaghy, you will recall, is the NBA referee who bet on NBA games in which he officiated, as well as provided inside information to gamblers so that they could place bets based on his information. Donaghy pleaded guilty and served a 15-month sentence (should have been 15 years) for felony wire fraud charges. Donaghy, out walking amongst us now, has recently released his book (ghost-written?) called *Personal Foul*—and it is certainly a "personal foul." His accusations and impeachment of fellow officials is disgraceful. A rat turns on others to save himself. Further, Donaghy incriminates coaches, players, and supervisors with accusations that often are not substantiated by fact.

With my four decades of officiating, this crime hit me right in the pit of my stomach. Ouch! Not only would I never even think of such debauchery, but never have witnessed it with any of my officiating colleagues.

Donaghy claims "addiction" (to gambling) as a great part of his problem. Hogwash! While some may have "gambling addictions," a sense of honor, justice, and *just do the right thing* would/should overtake such compulsions. The words "greed" and "easy money" are more often the case, rather than addiction. Donaghy crossed a line he never should have been near.

In *On My Honor, I Will,* author Pennington discusses several characteristics that define integrity, and then asks the reader to rate (1-to-5 scale) him/herself. Here are just a couple: "I know what I stand for." "I make decisions based on what's right for all parties." I wonder how Donaghy would rate himself on those traits.

    Will you "On Your Honor" practice good for others?

September 20, 2010

After further review …

So, Reggie Bush has volunteered to return his Heisman Trophy. I guess "volunteered" is the *right* word, even though the Heisman board decided not to "take it away." Think Bush acted too hastily? You will recall that #25 was awarded (never did like the word "won") the Heisman Trophy for his stellar athleticism as a running back for USC (University of Southern California) during the 2005 football season. Bush did the "right thing" by returning his trophy. He claims returning it "was not any admission of guilt." Hmmm…

Bush was found guilty by the NCAA for violating its rules during his tenure at USC. The NCAA discovered that Bush and his family received "hundreds of thousands of dollars in gifts" from two California-based marketing agents. The Heisman board "requires players to be in good standing with the NCAA," who chastised Bush, as well as putting the USC football program on probation. This is the first time in the 75-year Heisman Trophy history than an awardee has forfeited his trophy. Shameful for the Heisman. Shameful for Bush. Shameful for the storied football program at USC. Shameful for the university. Shameful for the game of football.

Too many of our "sports stars" have created indiscretions. As an example, in today's MLB, McGwire, Bonds, Rose, Conseco, and Clemens certainly raise questions of outstanding on-field athletic performance versus off-field improprieties. And then there is the case of O.J. Simpson—need I say more?

So what about Bush? Will the College Football Hall of Fame deny his induction, when he becomes eligible? And what of USC? Questions abound about how all this could happen under the (supposedly) watchful eye of USC's athletic department, with a dozen+ football coaches and athletic advisors. That notwithstanding, it is still the responsibility of the athlete himself to maintain his integrity, as well as uphold the honor of his university. That is where Bush failed himself—and all of us.

Bush now sounds remorseful, saying he wants to make amends to USC and its football program and asks "How do I clear my name?" How about this: Bush sits down with a trusted media person and tells the whole story—"cleansing" himself, so to speak. Further, since Bush is making millions by playing for the New Orleans Saints, he could make a sizable donation to the USC athletic program to provide scholarships for others. Bush needs to demonstrate the honorableness within.

 Will you support Bush if he makes amends and follows these suggestions?

After further review …

The 145th running of the Belmont Stakes provided thoroughbred racing fans with yet another surprise as Palace Malice upset both Oxbow (the Preakness winner) and Orb (the Kentucky Derby winner), who finished second and third respectfully. Two national Racing Hall of Fame jockeys, Mike Smith aboard Palace Malice and Gary Stevens atop Oxbow, raced neck-and-neck as they rounded the final turn, both driving their horses to win.

In that final rush for the finish, when Stevens saw that Palace Malice was hard-charging past his mount, he said to Smith, "You go on with him big boy, you're moving faster than me." Was Stevens giving up? Was he conceding the race before it was over? Not on your life. Stevens is in the Hall of Fame, not only for his racing record (nearly 12,000 victories), but also in recognition of his integrity. He has been a jockey for over 30 years and has won the Kentucky Derby, the Preakness Stakes, and the Belmont Stakes three times each, as well as eight Breeders Cups. He is considered a class act in the racing world.

In the Belmont race, Stevens, with such vast experience, knew his mount Oxbow didn't have "it" that day and made an honorable gesture to a fellow Hall-of-Famer with his words of encouragement. Do jockeys talk to each other as they race along as 45-plus mph? You bet they do; although the language sometimes used is not printable here. How do I know that?

Well, for starters, my father, Jim Sr., was a thoroughbred racing official for 20 years at California race tracks. Dad was recruited to that job in the mid-1940s, when horse racing was earning a bad reputation due to alleged "fixing" of races by jockeys, trainers, and/or owners. Dad had never ridden a horse, but being a top-notch sports official, knew a foul when he saw one and never failed to call it. My younger brother, Peter, has been in the racing business for over 50 years, with more than 30 of those years as general manager of a northern California track, by maintaining that same level of integrity.

But this is not so much about them as it is about the courage and honor of jockey Stevens. In the heat of battle, during one of the premier horse races in the world, the tested old veteran had the wherewithal to encourage a fellow competitor. We don't see much of that in today's sports world.

 Will you show honor and dignity to others in your competitive environment?

7 INTEGRITY

After further review …

NASA recently terminated astronaut Lisa Nowak, a U.S. Navy captain. Although never employed by NASA (National Aeronautics and Space Administration), she was on loan from the Navy. Why is that newsworthy? People are fired every day—ask Donald Trump.

NASA said it has "no good alternatives to keep her on board with the pending criminal charges against her." Nowak, called "the diaper lady," drove nonstop from Houston to Miami in Depends® to stalk and attempt to kidnap the girlfriend of a former lover. Captain Nowak is charged with attempted kidnapping, burglary, and battery. She pleaded "not guilty" of course.

While this "love triangle" is in Dr. Phil's ballpark—not mine—it does have an issue that relates to "my ballpark"—the world of sports. And that is: If NASA can "fire" her (terminated is the proper term) when she wasn't an employee and is only charged (not convicted), could/should that happen to professional athletes? If appears that NASA is very interested in and concerned with the integrity of its program involving "conduct unbecoming" and feels its integrity has been compromised. I agree.

Would this firing be effective in the world of professional sports? It could; however, some will scream "discrimination," "profiling," and "presumption of innocence." NASA is saying this type of alleged crime *will not be tolerated.*

Within days of the Nowak termination, an NFL team fired its assistant coach after "his arrest in a prostitution sting." Well, what about the number of NFL players arrested for felonies during the 2006 season? In the case of players, the NFL teams must deal with the NFLPA (National Football League Players Association) C.B.A. (Collective Bargaining Agreement). Coaches are not included in that C.B.A.

My concern is "rights" versus "responsibility." If an alleged felon has rights, so does the organization. Do we too often protect the "alleged" criminal and overlook protecting the teams and league—and the fans? Playing professional sports is a privilege, not a right.

Let's look at this scenario: What if, when a professional player is charged with a felony, he/she is immediately suspended. If the sport is "in season," he/she could not play until the case was adjudicated. The point is to protect not only the image of professional sports, but also its integrity. It is the hope and intent here that the league and players' association work more closely together to ensure that the integrity of the game is first and foremost.

 Will you make "integrity" your personal responsibility in all that you do?

October 8, 2007

After further review …

The year of 2007 may be recorded in history as one focusing on sports officials, e.g., bribery, scandal, and prejudice. Early in the year, a story in the *New York Times* claimed that there was prejudice in calling fouls in the NBA. It was reported, "white NBA referees called fouls at a greater rate against black players than against white players." The study said there was a "subconscious prejudice" afoot. The study was later found to be not only inaccurate but also racially damaging (see "On the Tunney Side of the Street," May 7, 2007).

Then, as the NBA playoffs were concluding in June 2007, the FBI reported that Tim Donaghy, a 13-year NBA referee, was under investigation for "bribery and controlling the over/under point spread." Donaghy has resigned and the investigation is at the point of indictment.

In August 2007, a study out of Texas reported that Major League baseball umpires vary their ball/strike count depending on the color of the batter. Two questions come to mind: 1) has the writer of this story ever put on a mask and chest protector and stood behind a catcher to call balls and strikes? And 2) the technology in MLB today is so refined—and reviewed—that an umpire has little or no chance to influence a "count" on a consistent basis.

I guess the follow-up question would be, why? Why would anyone jeopardize his professional livelihood to risk that? And for what purpose? Does the word greed come to mind?

The Donaghy saga often has been a suspicion by fans. When their team loses, they look to find fault with 1) the officials; 2) the rules, 3) the coach; and 4) yes, occasionally the player(s).

In today's world of insider trading e.g., Enron, Tyco, and Adelphia, etc., nothing is beyond suspicion. Can we place enough "checks and balances" to eliminate these scams? Sarbanes-Oxley attempts to do that, but falls short of people's susceptibility to greed and power.

In the last week of the 2007 MLB season, the MLB commissioner Bud Selig suspended umpire Mike Winter for using profanity. Winter had ejected the player who then challenged the umpire. Winter lost his "cool" and used profanity. When questioned by the commissioner, Winter admitted he had used profanity. His admission was the right thing to do.

Sports officials are more visible, more scrutinized by fans than ever before. They are responsible for the integrity of the game. Their behavior, their leadership can—and must be—an example for others to follow.

 Will you place "always doing the right thing" as your top priority?

After further review …

"Happy birthday, Dad!" Mark said as he crossed home plate on September 7, 1998, after hitting his 61st home run, tying the Major League home run record. Yes, Mark is Mark McGwire, former St. Louis Cardinals' first baseman. McGwire, who had a Hall of Fame career (16 years), Rookie of the Year (1987), Golden Glove award (1991), All Century team (1999)—was paying tribute to his father John, a retired dentist, who was in attendance. John had poliomyelitis in his youth (age seven, circa 1944) and was never able to realize his potential of pursuing his career in baseball.

Unfortunately, for father John and mother Ginger, son Mark (one of five boys) has recently fallen from grace with the admission of his use of performance-enhancing drugs (PEDs). McGwire, in a recent television interview, said his use of steroids did not contribute to his ability to hit home runs. PA-lease!

While we don't know all there is to know about how the use of PEDs improves a player's skill, the real issue is the illegality in the world of sports. We can easily cite cases of Lyle Alzado (deceased Raiders' DE), Ben Johnson (Olympic sprinter), and many others who used steroids, causing Johnson to be stripped of his medals and contributing to Alzado's death. What is more important is the integrity of the game. Although baseball fans love to see home run barrages, would fans admire a player's skills, if they knew their "slugger" was cheating? I think not. Goose Gossage, a HOF pitcher said, "There is no place in Cooperstown (location of the MLB Hall of Fame) for any player who uses PEDs." Reggie Jackson (1993 HOF), aka Mr. October, says he is "hurt" by McGwire's revelation; #44's hurt is the "hurt" the use of steroids puts on the game.

Is the steroid-era in the MLB over? MLB commissioner Bud Selig says it is; others aren't so sure. The issue here is not so much about McGwire's HOF eligibility or when the "era" is over; the issue is about "cheating." How do we teach young and current athletes that you can't cheat your way into fame?

Take time to read *Sixty Feet, Six Inches,* a recently released book by Bob Gibson and Reggie Jackson, both Hall of Famers. Steroids? Peds? Cheating? Those thoughts would never enter their minds.

Will you maintain the integrity of any game you play by not circumventing its rules?

June 21, 2010

After further review …

"A moment of silence," the announcer said as the crowd quieted to recognize the passing of Coach John Wooden. "A moment of silence" is hardly enough for this giant of a coach who took basketball to an extraordinary level. While Wooden disliked the moniker—Wizard of Westwood—he did, indeed, deserve the highest praise for his accomplishments. His famous quote, "Be quick, but don't hurry," is echoed by many.

Coach Wooden personally meant a lot to me. My basketball coaching days were few—only four seasons at an East Los Angeles high school. We didn't have any six+ foot players on the T.E.A.M., so I attended every clinic where Wooden spoke, and adopted his backcourt pressure defense. Using a "trap defense," we achieved two league titles, one of which was an undefeated season.

When I was a 26-year-old aspiring basketball official, Coach Wooden recommended me to the Pacific Coast Conference—now called the Pac 10. Wooden was in the stands at a Los Angeles city schools championship game scouting players and came to our official's room after the game. He congratulated us on a "good game," and then said to me, "If I may, Jim, I'd like to recommend you to officiate in our (PCC) league." Wow! What a break in my officiating career.

That invitation began my 11-year tenure as a PCC basketball official, with many good things to come. I was assigned to officiate the first game when UCLA opened Pauley pavilion. When Power Memorial Academy's Lewis Alcindor chose UCLA, many accused Wooden, and UCLA, of unfair recruiting. Lewis (later to be known as Kareem Abdul Jabbar) was a straight-A high school student and continued that academic prowess at UCLA. In addition, he was a three-year All American (67 to 69)—twice Player of the Year, with 88 wins and two losses in three years. I worked many of those games, as well as the game with freshmen Alcindor (1965), when his frosh team beat the varsity 75 to 60 at Pauley.

My admiration for Wooden's style of coaching did not allow him any concessions. I took pride in my officiating to "call 'em as I seen 'em"—Wooden notwithstanding. Did he yell at me? Of course, but *never, never* any profanity. "Goodness gracious, sakes alive" were his famous "cuss words." And yes, there were a few occasions when, as referee, I had to insist that he "sit down coach!"—a command to which he always complied.

Following those 11 years of PCC officiating, he and I became friends off the court, hopefully, I believe, built on an earned mutual respect.

 Will you maintain your integrity to develop a mutual respect with others?

After further review ...

The 2010 World Cup of Soccer brought to light—again—the integrity of the game. There were a number of missed calls—"blown calls" is the term used more often. Were these calls missed by the officials because of 1) incompetence; 2) not being in the right position; or 3) was there *any* semblance of prejudice on the part of the officials?

When former NBA referee Tim Donaghy—a 13-year veteran—was found guilty of "bribery and controlling the point spread" a couple years ago, the whole idea of cheating by game officials raised the question. Donaghy's crime hit me right in the pit of my stomach.

A study out of Texas reported that Major League baseball umpires vary their ball/strike count depending on the color of the batter—that's totally unacceptable. Three questions come to mind: 1) how credible is that report? 2) did the writer of that story ever put on a mask and chest protector and stand behind a catcher? and 3) the technology in MLB today is so refined—and reviewed—that an umpire has little or no chance to influence a "count" on a consistent basis. Why would anyone jeopardize his professional livelihood to risk that?

In today's world of corporate corruption, e.g., Enron, Tyco, Madoff, Adelphia, etc., nothing is beyond suspicion. Can we place enough "checks and balances" to eliminate these scams? Sarbanes-Oxley attempts to do that, but falls short of people's susceptibility to greed and power.

A MLB umpire was suspended a few seasons back for using profanity. He had ejected the player who then challenged the umpire. The umpire lost his "cool" and used profanity. When questioned by the commissioner, the umpire admitted he had used profanity. His admission was the right thing to do. That incident brought to mind a recent column I wrote about Doug Harvey. What impressed me about Harv and others with whom I officiated was that when an umpire has strong self-confidence, respects players and coaches, knows the rules and does what is fair, an outrage by a player or coach is better understood—not tolerated—just understood.

Sports officials are more visible, more scrutinized by fans, players, and coaches than ever before. They must understand that they are responsible for the integrity of the game. Their behavior, their leadership can—and must be—an example for others.

 Will you place "always doing the right thing" as your top priority?

After further review …

DYKWIAM! Some sports stars, heritage and/or background notwithstanding, when confronted by law enforcement personnel, all-too-often say "DYKWIAM," meaning "Don't you know who I am?" This is taken to mean "I am a super star and you, officer, need to leave me alone." While this is not a recent occurrence with Barry, Kobe, or Tiger, the attitude displayed by each conveys the DYKWIAM feeling.

Barry, of course, is Barry Bonds, who has been convicted of "obstruction of justice by a federal jury involving the use of (PED) performance-enhancing drugs." The jury was deadlocked on many of the other charges since, according to the report, the "evidence was not conclusive." While the indictment of "obstruction of justice" may be appealed, the testimony of his "use" resulted in a series of evasive answers"—no conviction.

The point here is not the jury trial, but that the feds should have never been involved in the first place. If Major League baseball, under the direction of Commissioner Bud Selig et al. had done its job, the whole mess of the jury trial might have been avoided. It might have been better being adjudicated within baseball itself. Barry is not alone in the use of PEDs. If MLB had done some serious drug testing, perhaps, Roger Clemens, Jose Canseco, Mark McGwire, Sammy Sosa, and others could have avoided that scandal.

The issue of DYKWIAM with Kobe (Bryant) is his excessive use of foul language and the berating of an NBA referee using an anti-gay epithet. If you have ever sat at courtside or close to it during an NBA game, you can hear foul language used constantly. But Kobe, who has since apologized, is the face of the NBA today and must set an example. His fine of $100,000 and suspension of two games next season is a slap in the face of discipline. Next season? If the offence is that serious, why isn't it immediate?

Tiger's (Woods) DYKWIAM is more about his haughtiness, which certainly caught up with him in November of 2009. While it appears his immortality issue is in remission, Tiger still has not improved his on-the-course demeanor. Thousands of kids who took up the game, because of Tiger, watch his every action and copy what they see. Those who attain a professional status in sports must hold themselves to a higher standard by displaying an elevated level of integrity and morals.

 Will you expect (and practice) only the best of yourself in those areas?

After further review …

From the time I was playing on the Washington grammar school playground, all the way to being part of Super Bowl XI at the Rose Bowl in Pasadena, California, I admired and wanted to be the best I could be. It wasn't an effort to be better than others; it was just to be the best my God-given talent would allow me to be. Along that journey, I admired those athletes who had achieved greatness at the college or professional level. It wasn't stardom I was after. How *those* athletes achieved their success and the dedication and discipline they possessed was the path I wanted to follow.

As I followed my dream, it was the game of baseball that most attracted me, and while I never achieved much in that sport beyond college, the ambition to be the best I could be stayed with me. I still admire those who achieve at the higher levels. However, I learned to avoid those whose integrity didn't live up to the standards I expected of them or of myself.

The wave of suspensions currently forming in MLB's Biogenesis scandal troubles me. If, as reported in the media, baseball stars including Alex Rodriguez, the 2011 National League MVP—Ryan Braun, Cy Young Award winner—Bartolo Colon, and 2012 All Star MVP—Melky Cabrera, among others, are found (or re-found, in some cases) culpable of violating MLB's substance policies, it may do more damage to baseball than the 1919 World Series "Black Sox" scandal.

If the aforementioned do incur the toughened 100-game suspensions, America's grand game will be dealt a serious blow. And it won't be just to those players found guilty, but to the integrity of the sport and to the thousands of young players who admire what these players have accomplished. The latest phase of this exhausting controversy begs the question: just how important is *winning*, if gained through illegal means? Do our young athletes believe that *an extra* boost is needed to achieve a higher level?

The intent here is not to ignore the due process and assign blame. But it can't be overstated how crucial it is for talented athletes to understand that what they do and how they do it sends a message to others. They do have a responsibility for that.

 Will you maintain a strong sense of integrity in whatever you do?

8 JUDGMENT

After further review …

Lots of "sparks" at AT&T Park in San Francisco on August 7, 2007. The sparks were in the form of cameras, cell phones, and asterisks. The asterisks (*) were in response to Barry Bonds, San Francisco Giants' outfielder, who at 8:51 p.m. PDT, set the all-time Major League baseball home run record at #756 with his blast of 435 feet of a five-ounce ball, sending it into the centerfield bleachers.

"Whew! Glad that's over," you say. Well, not quite. Bonds continues to play for the Giants—they have 50+/- games left, then the playoffs—oops! Sorry—no playoffs for the Giants in 2007. But that night—8/7/07—was a memorable one, with Willie Mays in the park to congratulate his Godson.

Hank Aaron, Braves (both Milwaukee and Atlanta) outfielder for 22 years (1954-1976), who held the record of 755 (since 1976), was not in the park, but sent a message via the Jumbotron to Bonds. Classic Aaron—and a very classy message. MLB commissioner Bud Selig also was not present, as he was "taking care of business" by meeting with George Mitchell, the head of the MBL steroid investigation team.

Should have Selig been there? Difficult for the commissioner to be at every record-setting game. However, some say it is the commissioner's resentment of Bonds breaking Aaron's record that kept him away. Or perhaps the "steroid cloud" hanging over Bonds' head caused the commissioner's reluctance to be supportive. The beauty of Aaron as a player was that you didn't even know he was on the field. With Bonds, all eyes watch his every move.

While I applaud individual achievements, I am more inclined to see those efforts go toward a T*E*A*M accomplishment. What may have been overlooked at or about 9:00 p.m. on August 7 was that Bonds' 756th home run gave the Giants a 5-4 lead. Unfortunately, the Giants lost on this historic night 8-6 to the Washington Nationals.

That ever-present "cloud" has to do, of course, with the allegations that Bonds used performance-enhancing drugs. Before we place that asterisk next to #756 (Bonds hit #757 the next night—and maybe more before you read this), we must ask two questions: 1) Is he guilty—i.e., did he really use those drugs?; and 2) If he did use them, were MLB laws in place to prohibit those performance-enhancing drugs? Of course, if Bonds did use drugs/steroids, etc., the consequences will eventually take their toll. I'll leave it up to you.

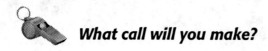 *What call will you make?*

After further review …

Is Michael Vick a role model? Or perhaps the verb needs to be "was," as in was Michael Vick a role model? Vick, as you are aware, pleaded guilty to several charges associated with "dog fighting," and, as a result, has been suspended from the NFL. The reference to his being a "role model," obviously, concerns his accomplishments as a football star (#7) with the Atlanta Falcons. Let's look at a definition of role model.

The word "model" is defined as "something worthy of copying." Is Vick's prowess as the Falcons' quarterback worthy of copying? How do you "copy" that kind of athleticism? Vick's ability to scramble out of the pocket (over 1000 yards in 2006) was something to be admired, of course, but unable to "copy." You can't "copy" talent. There are athletic moves that are hard to learn and even hard to do. There are athletic moves that are hard to learn and easy to do. Then, there are athletic moves that are easy to learn, but if you can't remember how or when you learned them—that's called talent.

Vick was a talented football player. There is some difficulty here calling Vick an athlete. In addition to God-given talent, an athlete incorporates the qualities of trustworthiness, respect, caring, fairness, responsibility, and citizenship. Those traits embody the word "character." In evaluating Vick's "character," we must ask: Did he practice those traits? Were they evident to others?

As Vick's case is adjudicated, it is with sincere hope and faith that he is judged on his behavior and not on his race, his environment, parental, teachers'/coaches' influence (or lack thereof), or on the influence of his "friends." Let's attribute Vick's behavior to his choices. If we admired the choices he made on the field as a quarterback, then we must place his off-field choices squarely on him—no one else.

When Vick appeared on national television to make a public statement in response to his guilty plea, he said, "First of all, I want to apologize for all the things I have done." I have done? As in "yes, I did commit all those crimes?" I wish he had also said, "I'd like to apologize for all the things I have not done." Things like: "doing the right thing," "obeying the law," "not allowing myself to associate with others of questionable character," and "not living up to the responsibilities I have to my family, the Falcons, my fans, and my teammates." That's the new Michael Vick we hope will emerge.

 Will you accept full responsibility for your behavior?

After further review …

"Twenty-three months in federal prison and three years probation," said federal judge Henry Hudson to defendant Michael Vick, former star quarterback of the Atlanta Falcons. Vick responded, "I'm willing to deal with the consequences and accept responsibility for my actions." Thanks, but too late, Mr. Vick.

Vick's crime and punishment is for lying about his involvement in the killing of 66 dogs—34 of them pit bulls. The actual killing of dogs, as well as other inhumane acts of torture included electrocution, drowning, strangulation, and barbarous training (for fighting).

In a statement released after his sentencing, Vick apologized to the NFL, Atlanta Falcons' owner, coaches and teammates, and to his family. Curiously, he made no apology to the dogs. One wishes that, in his contriteness, Vick would have apologized for the maltreatment of animals.

The question lingers: "Why?" How did Vick get himself in a position that would cost him imprisonment? And, incidentally, speaking of "costs," Vick stands to lose about $141 million in salary and endorsements.

Should Vick, #1 pick in the 2001 NFL draft, three-time Pro-Bowl selection in six seasons with the Falcons, play again in the NFL? Commissioner Roger Goodell, who suspended Vick in July 2007, said he will make no decision until the prison sentence has been served. Falcons' owner Arthur Blank said, "As an organization, we have to look forward and assume Michael will not be back."

The concern here is not about Vick as an NFL player, but as a human being. Yes, he still is that even though he did not offer that same humaneness to his dogs. Vick will be 30 years of age when his sentence is completed. Federal prison confinement usually doesn't offer NFL training table food or a training camp environment conducive to NFL conditioning.

Vick's difficulty started with "choices." While occasionally one's success happens by chance, I believe the future is determined by what choices one makes. It's up to each of us to make good choices, yet too often we are influenced by "friends," and many times those friends are in it for their personal gain, not yours. Vick involved himself with the wrong people.

Did Vick know right from wrong? Of course he did. Did his friends know what they were doing was illegal? Of course they did. Did Vick think that with all his money and fame that he could "get out of any trouble?" Perhaps.

 Will you think carefully about making good choices for your life's direction?

July 7, 2008

After further review …

The 2008 Olympic Games open one month from tomorrow, 08-08-08, in Beijing, China, with a lot of excitement and anticipation that the USA will be triumphant over our competitive countries. While I fully support our athletes and want them to do well, it appears to me—it has for many Olympic Games now—that we have let the "spirit" of the Olympics get away from us.

"Citius, Altius, Fortius"—interpreted to mean swifter, higher, stronger—has always been the Olympic motto. The games were designed to compare *individual athleticism*—not country competition. Most countries (not just the USA) want to "stack up" their country's scores against other countries (i.e., country versus country, not athlete versus athlete). The Olympic creed of "the essential thing is not to have conquered, but to have fought well" has been lost.

Enter the U.S. Olympic men's basketball T.E.A.M., being a team sport in itself takes away from the individual competition. Now, don't get ahead of me here—I like the T.E.A.M. concept and countries should put their best team forward. But the U.S. Olympic men's basketball T.E.A.M. is made up of NBA players—professionals!

You may recall that the great athlete Jim Thorpe had his Olympic gold medals in the decathlon and pentathlon 1912 Olympics taken away because it was later discovered that Thorpe had played on, and received money from, a professional baseball team. In today's Olympic competition, most of the players from every country are paid. USA began playing professionals in the Olympics when it was discovered we were sending our best amateur players, but facing professionals from other countries.

We should send our best athletes, but why not our best amateurs to maintain the "spirit" of the games. Sixteen years ago, the first *"Dream Team"* comprised of NBA players wanted five-star treatment by living in luxurious hotels and not in the Olympic Village. Granted, the Olympic Village was "Spartan" compared to what these professional athletes were used to, but the value of being together in an Olympic environment was lost—and so did the Dream Team.

Further, the selection of Denver Nugget's star Carmelo Anthony to the Olympic basketball team is suspect. Anthony certainly is one of the more talented players. However, the Nuggets suspended "Melo" for two games, starting the 2008-2009 NBA season, when he was recently arrested after "pleading guilty to driving while impaired" (DUI). If the Nuggets felt it necessary to take this aggressive action, why didn't the Olympic team do likewise? In sending our "best athletes," it is important to incorporate character along with athleticism.

 Will you support the Olympic Games that comprise the best amateurs strong in character, as well as athleticism?

December 7, 2009

After further review ...

My parents taught me about boundaries (i.e., being careful not to offend others through your words or actions). In any relationship (e.g., husband/wife, parent/child, teacher/student, etc.), each of us must respect the other person's space.

As an NFL official for 31 years, I practiced that both on and off the field. Some coaches and players wanted to be more than just friendly. However, it was important not to invade their space or allow them into mine. On the field, it's easy for an official to be familiar with coaches and players more than just as casual acquaintances. As an example, it is natural for an official to want to compliment a player when witnessing a great play—but you can't.

So when I saw an NFL official give a player a "high five," after that player solidified his team's victory in a Monday Night Football game, I was concerned. The high five occurred without the official initiating it, nor intending to give the impression he was congratulating the player. When it drew criticism, the bloggers went crazy. One blogger said, "It was funny and spontaneous; the sort of feel-good moment that's becoming all too rare in an increasingly humorless NFL."

Funny? To whom? It's not funny to the losing team or their fans. Officials must demonstrate impartiality to engender the trust of players, coaches, and fans. For example, if a coach approached me to shake hands when I walked on the field during pre-game preparation, I always went to the other coach to do the same. The first coach might just have wanted to say "hello," yet to others, it may appear to have been more than that. Be friendly, certainly; but, detached.

An official in any sport, at any level, must be sensitive to impartiality. At the pro level, there are millions of gambling dollars bet every day. With the conviction of (former) NBA official Tim Donaghy for providing information to gamblers, the risk level has been too "high." When Cincinnati Bengals #85 WR Ochocinco thought it was funny to try to stick a dollar bill in an official's pocket, he violated not just a rule (NFL fined him $20,000), but a boundary. In the recent Tiger Woods accident/transgression admission, the pubic may be fascinated; however, Woods has no responsibility for an explanation to the public. Boundaries apply universally.

 Will you respect the boundary of others by using good judgment?

After further review …

"The NFL doesn't care about their active players and they despise the retired players. All they offer is lip service to those with serious, life-challenging head injuries." Pretty serious accusations from many fans, as well as former players. This alleged lack of concern about player injuries is not new, but not necessarily cogent.

Going back as far as the leather helmet era, you could justifiably say there were significant head injuries among players in those days. Trouble is that in those days, we didn't have the technology that's available today to detect concussions. With the advent of the plastic helmet, the idea was that that type of helmet would protect the wearer. Sorry, didn't happen.

Didn't happen because with that "added protection," players began using their helmets as weapons to block and tackle. Coaches and players often disregard proper blocking and tackling techniques by "just throw your body in there" to block or tackle; some call that *terminator football*. That was not the way football was played in the 1960s, 70s, or 80s. Oh sure, it was a tough, physical game then, but a player would drive his shoulder into an opponent, and then wrap his arms around to tackle him. Why the change? Today's players are faster, bigger, and stronger with many being 6'6", 6'7"+, weighing 260 to 280+ pounds, and colliding with opponents who are of equal or greater size and strength.

Is the NFL really concerned about injuries, especially concussions? Of course they are. Officials are concerned too. One of the major responsibilities of the on-field officials is to protect players from unwarranted injuries. The rules can't legislate speed or power, but they can help reduce injuries. Here's a thought. How about removing the facemask? With the facemask-cage-type protection, players more often stick their head into an opponent, rather than use their shoulder for blocking and tackling.

While NFL commissioner Goodell and team owners want to help former players who now suffer headaches, dementia, and other head injuries, it becomes difficult to determine when and how such injuries occurred. Was it in high school or college that the player first suffered a head injury? Then, too, perhaps you know of people who have severe headaches (e.g., migraines, etc.) who never played football, perhaps falling as a young person that may have initially caused the injury. More needs to be done. Let's hope that the year 2010 will bring more help to those former players in need.

 Will you encourage the NFL to continue their efforts in reducing serious injuries?

After further review …

Choosing a college/university can be an emotional decision—and well it should be. For 16-, 17-, or 18-year-olds to leave the comfort of their home environment and move into an unknown world can be an unsettling adventure. How does one decide what is the best school environment? So many factors to consider.

Now, place yourself in the shoes (and head) of a "blue chipper" (i.e., one who excelled in athletics in high school and is now being recruited by some of the most prestigious colleges/universities in our country). What criteria should a young athlete use to determine which school is best?

As a high school teacher, coach, and administrator, I made it a thoughtful effort to guide every student toward the college that was the best fit. In the world of a "blue chipper" athlete, the matrix becomes more involved. Many athletes look to a college that is nationally ranked in that athlete's sport. Can you blame that attitude? Why wouldn't one want to play for a college T.E.A.M. that may position him/her to move onto the professional level?

Where, then, does educational value come into play? Hopefully, it should rank high in one's criteria. All too often, not high enough. One's purpose for going to college may have many avenues.

The National Football League requires that a player must attend three years of college—or at least wait three years after high school graduation—to be eligible for the NFL draft. Yes, you read correctly—an athlete does not have to go to college; but then, what advancement can be made on his playing skills if he doesn't? In the National Basketball Association, a player must be 19 before he is eligible for the NBA draft. If he graduates high school at 18 years of age, he must attend at least one year of college (called "one and done") or just sit out a year until age 19.

Therefore, in the NFL or NBA, what is an athlete's purpose or goal in attending college? Is it just preparing him for a professional career? What classes must he enroll and attend, if his only purpose is playing professional sports? If this is the criteria in the selection of a college, where does the value of the coach rank? A highly successful college T.E.A.M. headed by a highly successful charismatic coach is awfully appealing to an 18-year-old.

 Will you carefully consider educational value when choosing a college?

February 15, 2010

After further review …

Should the victory by the New Orleans Saints in the Super Bowl diminish what most people say about Indianapolis Colts' quarterback Peyton Manning that he may be the "best of all time?"

I always have difficulty with those types of opinions: "Best of all time." My difficulty stems from the many changes that have occurred during the 50 years of my involvement with the NFL.

Let's take the best quarterback question. Technology and equipment have made a huge difference. My concern is about the various conditions players faced. Manning has demonstrated an excellent knowledge of the game and superb ability to "read" defenses. However, so did Starr, Unitas, Montana, Young, Staubach, and Jurgensen, as well as many others.

In today's NFL game, when play ends, the 40-second play clock starts; for 25 of those seconds, the quarterback is receiving information through an audio headset in his helmet—which play to call, defensive alignment, etc. Quarterbacks of the past didn't have that technological help. In fact, I watched Washington Redskins' quarterback Sonny Jurgensen diagram a play in the dirt, like we used to do as kids on the sandlot.

Emmitt Smith's performance as a Dallas Cowboys running back (1990-2002) produced outstanding rushing numbers. How does former HOF Cleveland Browns running back Jim Brown (1957-1965) compare? Consider this: In 1967, the NFL changed its blocking rules whereby an offensive player could use his hands and arms extended to block or push an opponent. In Brown's day, offensive players had to keep their hands at or near their chest and block opponents only with their shoulders and/or body.

Jerry Rice is arguably the best wide receiver there ever was. Jerry, and this is not to take anything away from his performance, had the opportunity to wear gloves. Those gloves had "grips" on the fingers that enable today's receivers to more easily catch a pass. Receivers in other days didn't have gloves. Times, equipment, and rules have changed.

Finally, Manning threw an errant pass near the end of Super Bowl XLIV, which was intercepted and returned for a touchdown by the Saints' Tracy Porter to seal the victory. In Super Bowl XI, Minnesota's quarterback Fran Tarkenton experienced the same fate when Oakland Raiders' DB Willie Brown intercepted Tark's pass and ran 75 yards for a score with the Raiders winning 32-14. As Tarkenton left the field, he turned to me (as referee) and said, "I'll be back." So will Manning.

 Will you consider all factors when comparing athletes of different eras?

After further review …

The AP article by Doug Ferguson carried this headline: *Masters' Chairman Lashes Out at Woods* (as in Tiger). Augusta national chairman Billy Payne said, "Our hero did not live up to the expectations of the role model we saw for our children." Payne would not discuss the details of their (before the start of the 2010 Masters) meeting—called at Payne's request.

The article concluded with chairman Payne saying, "This year, it (the Masters) will not be just for him, but for all of us who believe in second chances." Why couldn't *that* be the headline instead of "lashes out?" What do we gain by beating up on others? If, indeed, Payne believes in second chances, why not focus on moving on?

Christine Brennan suggested in her *USA Today* column "Woods should yank his first tee shot into the trees and shoot 75. That would be the humane thing to do." Is Brennan expressing female anger at Tiger's infidelity? She certainly is entitled to her opinion, but, again, is it her plan to continue to berate him? Just asking.

Please understand that Tiger's behavior of infidelity is not to be—and cannot be—defended. He made serious mistakes over a long period of time, and has publicly admitted so saying, "It's my fault—no one else is to blame." With that admission, along with his therapy and personal commitment to correct his misbehavior, is it time to move on?

Regarding the "hero" tag (per chairman Payne), Tiger is not a hero; he is a superb golfer, and maybe "one of the best ever." A hero is one who rescues others from a disaster—for example, NYC firemen during 9/11. Payne may have misplaced his expectations.

A role model? Of course. We do have a right to place that label on our sports stars. Pros, as well as everyday golfers, would all like to have Tiger's golfing skills. However, sports stars need to model professional behavior off the course as well.

We expect a higher standard of our leaders; some of whom have failed us, as is the case of our 42nd President, the Ponzi scheme guy, and the Enron CEO—who have "cheated," as well. The infidelity issue that Tiger faces is a personal one with his wife, Erin, and his family. In the words of Ron Read, who will announce the golfers as each tees off in the 2010 U.S. Open at Pebble Beach, "Play away."

 Will you be able to follow Read's words of "play away" and move beyond Woods' tragic past?

After further review …

A 17-year-old named Steve ran across the outfield of Citizens Bank Ballpark in Philadelphia recently during a game between the St. Louis Cardinals and the Phillies. He was chased by three or four ballpark security and a uniformed cop. Unable to catch the intruder, the cop, from about 20 feet away, fired his taser gun and felled the culprit. The young man got to his feet, was taken into custody, and has recovered from the taser shot. Some are questioning the use of a taser in this situation.

My question is different, to wit: Where does it state on Steve's admission ticket that he had the right to be on the playing field—before, during, or after the game? What happened to modesty? Did his parents not teach that? Well, it turns out his mom, Amy, has since apologized for her son's conduct. Steve had actually called his father from the ballpark to tell him his intention, and the father told him "not to do it." Good advice, but not followed; wonder what part of "not" didn't he understand? Sounds like mom and dad tried to do the right thing. Steve knew he was "in the wrong" and perhaps just wanted his "15 minutes in the sun." I don't think that's what Andy Warhol had in mind. Now, I don't want to get into Dr. Phil's territory, but who is influencing this kid's behavior?

'Course this fan-on-the-field is not new. During my 31-year career on the NFL field, I've seen it, perhaps a dozen times. I've watched NFL players "deck" an intruder saying, "Hey buddy, you're interrupting my game." A wayward fan has got to be out of his mind to face an NFL player's confrontation.

Still the question lingers…to tase or not to tase? The Philadelphia police commissioner, after reviewing the tape, has supported the officer. Some critics of the use of a taser said, "Well, he was just running around the field, without harm to anyone." How did the officer know? Maybe if an officer would have tased that guy who came onto the tennis court in Hamburg Germany, he could have prevented Monica Seles from being stabbed in the back while she sat in her chair during a break in the Citizen Cup tournament.

 Will you support reasonable means to enforce the law?

After further review …

"If we don't win our last game, it's disappointing," said Detroit Tigers catcher Alex Avila. The Bosten Red Sox defeated the Tigers 5-2 in the sixth game of the American League Championship Series, sending the Red Sox on to the World Series to face the National League champion St. Louis Cardinals.

Avila used the word "disappointing" (which suggests that losing would be a failure to meet expectations) rather than the word "discouraging" (which by plain definition is a loss of confidence or enthusiasm). Avila concluded "I'm very proud of what we've done." There is little doubt that he and his teammates are looking forward to 2014— with spring training just a short four months away.

The Tigers have reason for high hopes in 2014. With talents such as Avila, Torrii Hunter, Miguel Cabrera (2012 MVP awardee), Anibal Sanchez (AL ERA champ), Max Scherzer (2011 Cy Young awardee), and Justin Verlander on the team, they figure to compete deep into the season. Respected veteran manager Jim Leyland has stepped down, but the team itself remains largely intact.

But how will the Tigers proceed all the way to the World Series? How would you? How does one deal with disappointment after working diligently for eight months in pursuit of a reachable goal? In the education and business worlds, many strive long and arduously without reaching valued goals. It is vital to remember that losing or failing is not a forever thing; giving up or quitting is!

"There's no quit in my dictionary," says ESPN analyst and former NFL player and coach Herm Edwards in the book *It's the Will, Not the Skill*. "Will" is the essential factor in the Tigers' (or anybody else's) prospects for success. Every MLB T*E*A*M intends to win the World Series. Yet it's the T*E*A*M with the full, pure power of *will* that is likely to prevail (though good pitching and hitting help, of course).

The adage "forget to remember" helps one to let go of past disappointments. When you realize that beating yourself up is wasted energy, then you are able to move forward with a new and enthusiastic plan. Possessing the will to execute it is a positive step toward success. It's the *plan* that lays the groundwork for success, so we can do some further refining; the *will* to prepare is more important than the will to win!

 Will you make preparation the keystone as you set your next goal?

October 11, 2010

After further review …

When I heard recently that executive VP and general manager Omar Minaya and manager Jerry Manuel of the New York Mets were fired, it didn't strike me as unusual. I mean, general managers and head coaches, if you will, are fired on a regular basis near or at the end of a season. Owners/CEOs certainly have a right to do that. However, the method/process of *this* termination is bothersome.

As I understood it, the announcement of these "firings" was broadcast on ESPN, with Minaya and Manuel not being personally informed. That's wrong! One of the reasons for labor unions, as well as teacher tenure (don't get me started) is because of these kinds of procedures.

Herm Edwards, local Monterey Peninsula football legend, states in my book, *It's the Will, Not the Skill*, that after nine full seasons playing for the Philadelphia Eagles, he was "released." That came in the form of an assistant coach coming by to pick up his playbook. The head coach, in his first year at the time, never even spoke to Edwards.

A decade later, when Edwards became the New York Jets head coach, he vowed that he would never release, trade, or fire a player or an assistant coach without a face-to-face discussion. Edwards walked his talk all eight years he was a head coach.

The 2010 television program, "Undercover Boss," highlighted some well-known companies, describing how the "boss" disguised himself as a beginning employee to work alongside his employees at their site location. In every case, the "boss" came away with a better understanding and appreciation for the job of that employee.

Many years ago, the term "M.B.W.A."—Management by Walking About—became the way to run a business. That philosophy decried the "M.B.I.T."—Management by Ivory Tower. It always seemed to me that "ya gotta get your hands dirty;" that is, do the hard work at some time to better understand the workings of your company and its employees.

Working *with* employees, rather than the employees working *for* you, engenders the kind of teamwork needed for a successful T.E.A.M. In fact, the term "manager" has always troubled me. It has been my belief that you "lead people" and manage things. Hard to change the baseball title manager to baseball leader (just wouldn't sound right), but that is what he is.

The title "leader" applies to a coach, principal, teacher, parent, or anyone empowered to guide others. Further, as my colleague Mark Sanborn says, "You don't have to have a title to be a leader."

 Will you be a leader or a manager?

After further review …

Trash talk: good or bad? Huh? Is that question even acceptable? Was trash talking a deciding factor in the New York Jets @ New England Patriots 2011 divisional game? Let's hope not. While the definition of "trash" has several variations, the ones that come to mind are: "something that is not good"; "matter that is regarded as worthless"; and synonyms such as garbage or junk, and the one that jumps out—riffraff—meaning mob.

Some may remember world boxing champ Muhammad Ali making it popular some 40 years ago. As a brash young boxer out of Louisville, known as Cassius Clay, he bragged about his boxing style with "floats like a butterfly, stings like a bee." Sounds kinda cute and harmless in today's vernacular, but in those days, that braggadocios talk offended many. Ali not only backed up his talk with his abilities, but as he grew older, became someone to be admired—a change welcomed by the sports world.

Today's players (it's difficult to call them "athletes") who so openly trash others, have taken TT to a new level—one of "rubbish." Please note that those of this ilk are not in the majority, although it may seem so. The few who do so give their T*E*A*M a hideous reputation. TT is not limited to sports. Certainly, politics comes to mind, and the media loves it. It sells newspapers and "talking heads" programs. Is TT damaging, and if so, to whom?

Young athletes have always desired to emulate their sports heroes (heroes is their term, not mine). First college, then grade school, then Little League players do what big brother (or sister) does, since that is the message they hear and see. Who can correct that poor behavior depicted by some players? Parents, of course, can help, but too often are overshadowed by the youths' peers and, further, see no harm in it.

Patriots' coach Bill Belichick showed the television and radio audience in an important divisional game by "sitting down," i.e., not starting, his star wide receiver Wes Welker for breaking the T*E*A*M's code of silence with his media response to the Jets' TT. That may set an example for all coaches in all sports to follow. Coaches/teachers more than anyone need to shoulder this responsibility.

 Will you keep civility alive by dissuading trash talking wherever and whenever you hear it?

After further review …

The European Golf Tour played recently in Dubai in the United Arab Emirates produced more than Spain's Alvaro Quiros as its champion. Unfortunately, for Quiros, the "breaking news" was Tiger Woods—not his golf, but his behavior. Following his missed putt on the 12th green, Woods spit (call it spittle, if you wish) on the green in disgust. "Upon further review," Mike Stewart of the Euro Tour fined Woods an undisclosed amount for his conduct. While the amount is insignificant, the offence (English version) was all over the media.

Woods' apology was immediate, "It was inconsiderate to spit like that and I know better—just wasn't thinking and I want to say I'm sorry." The apology was met with mixed responses. Some, without defending the behavior, mentioned that if it were not Tiger, it probably would not have drawn that kind of attention. Others, without much ado, just accepted the apology at face value.

The question arises do we accept that apology believing that Woods' act was one of just not thinking? Or do we continue to heap blame on him because of his infidelity (2009) that led to his world-famous divorce? Do we punish the behavior or the persona? My father's advice comes to mind about what he taught me regarding discipline: 1) what's best for the individual; 2) what's best for the group (others); and 3) what would you do if this were your own child?

First and foremost, spitting in public is unsightly and unhealthy. Yet, show me the guy who hasn't done it. However, when you engage in the game of golf, you automatically accept the rules of golf. Think it's possible to invoke that rule in Major League baseball? Ever seen a MLB dugout after a game? I've certainly seen spitting on the field in the NFL. How about soccer? Probably wouldn't happen in indoor sports.

Woods' action, although outdoors and disgusting, may cause golfers who follow to walk or putt through that spittle. So the question remains, do you find fault with the behavior of the individual? Some will never forgive Woods for his infidelity, as some will never forgive Philadelphia Eagles quarterback Michael Vick for his insolent treatment and killing of dogs (2007).

 Will you deal with the behavior of the persona when criticizing and/or disciplining others?

After further review …

Coaches often say that they would rather have a player who makes other players great, than a great player. Since many players fit that appellation, it would be inappropriate to mention some and risk omitting others.

With the 2011 March Madness still well in mind, this tournament did have players who made others on their T*E*A*M play better. It must be pointed out, however, that the championship game fell badly short of a great game. Yet, I couldn't help but notice the excellent quality of officiating throughout the tournament. Not one game was decided by an errant call by an official.

Yes, you might point out that the third round game between Butler and Pittsburgh had two calls in the last few seconds that Butler was able to convert and Pittsburgh wasn't. The first was poor judgment by a Butler player, only to be followed by a Pittsburgh player's error. Upon review of these two fouls, the calls by the officials were deemed worthy. John Adams, the NCAA supervisor of officials said later that if such a foul would be called at the beginning of a game, it must be called at the end.

Having officiated basketball at the college level for 25+ years, I have found that officiating a game as poorly played as this championship game was, it is always more difficult than one where both teams are playing well. The players want to play their best when a championship is on the line. That didn't happen in the 2011 game. Yet, let us not overlook that the crew of John Cahill (Big East), Verne Harris (Mountain West), and Doug Shows (SEC) that worked in championship form. Some might say that the best officiated games are those where the officials are not noticed. I disagree.

The teams that qualify for the Final Four had been playing together for many months, and one would expect that their togetherness would be well-honed. Those three officials not only don't work together often, they're not even from the same conference. Teams can have a "bad game." That is not acceptable in officiating. Everybody knows about it when it does. Well, please notice when a game, especially of championship magnitude, is well-officiated.

 Will you recognize good performance and be grateful for it?

After further review …

They're playing a game that's hard to watch anymore. This is in reference to the NBA (National Basketball Association) brand of what used to be called basketball. The game has changed a lot since Jimmy Naismith first hung his "peach baskets" on the railings of the Springfield (Mass.) YMCA. Of course, all sports taken to the professional level have changed—progress, well …?

Having "shot baskets" since my dad gave me my first basketball, then played and coached, as well as refereed the game for 50+ years, I have loved the strategies and techniques this game of finesse has provided. But, finesse no longer it is. The size of players from high school through college and into the pros has become gargantuan. When size, speed, and strength took over, finesse, ball-handling, and, yes, even teamwork departed.

There is (was?) a basic rule in basketball called "pivot foot," meaning that once a player gains possession of the ball and has both feet on the floor, he can move (only) one foot in any direction as many times as he wants as long as the pivot foot is fixed (i.e., stationary). That doesn't seem to apply in today's game. If and when you do move that pivot foot, you must bounce (dribble) the ball before your pivot foot hits the floor again. Failing to dribble as you move that foot is called traveling—nonexistent in today's game.

There is also a basic rule euphemistically called "palming" (or carrying) the ball when dribbling. This rule is designed to maintain that the ball is advanced (the other way is passing the ball) without the player simply running with the ball. Neither of these basic rules seems to be observed in today's game—each being a violation, not a foul. And speaking of fouls, this is where the term "shame game" applies.

Players today don't seem intent upon just blocking a shot, but in physically attacking their opponent who is shooting. NBA Hall of Famer and former L.A. Lakers' guard Jerry West was recently quoted as saying he was "embarrassed with some of the things he saw on the court that a Lakers player did." "Cheap shots" by Lakers Artest, Bynum, and Odom drew this criticism. This is not just true of the Lakers, but of *all* NBA teams.

 Will you continue to watch the NBA playoffs with this style of play being all too common?

After further review …

Catching a home run ball is usually no big deal—except for the fan who caught it. The home run ball hit by New York Yankees' captain Derek Jeter on July 9, 2011 was, indeed, a big deal. It was Jetter's 3000th hit. What a prize for that fan. However, what followed gives us hope for some sanity.

Christian Lopez, the fan who made that catch, is a 23-year-old cell phone salesman whose family is from Puerto Rico. Lopez did not hesitate in his decision with what to do with that special ball. He gave it back to Jeter. He what? That historic ball, by some people's estimation, might have sold for as much as $250,000. Could a cell phone salesman use that kind of money? What's the "deal" here (in New York, there's always a "deal")? Well, Lopez, a 6'5" former linebacker from New York's St. Lawrence University said, "Jeter's an icon. He deserves that ball. He worked hard for it."

Jeter, who hit the eighth pitch in the third inning off Tampa Bay Rays' pitcher David Price, was the *first* player in Yankees' history to reach 3000 hits. Wow! Considering Ruth, Gehrig, DiMaggio, Mantel, Maris, Jackson, et al., as his predecessors, it makes Jeter's home run ball even more valuable. While Jeter became the 28th player to reach that historic level, he is only the second player in MLB history to have his 3000th hit a homer; Wade Boggs being the first.

Lopez, sitting in the left field bleachers with his father (who first touched the ball but fumbled it), had received his $55 game ticket as a birthday gift from his girlfriend. Lopez not only received national attention, including a nine-minute TV interview, but offers for product endorsements followed. Yet, Lopez didn't expect any reward.

However, Yankees' management stepped up and gave him four tickets to a suite for every remaining Yankees' home game. Nice! Wait—just a minute. Now, "steps up big brother—the IRS—who will charge Lopez a $1400 tax liability for the gift. You kiddin' me? Lopez never considered keeping the ball nor did he request/demand a reward. What happened to common sense? Think the IRS would consider a waiver of this gift tax?

Will you show some gesture of kindness and generosity in what you do?

October 3, 2011

After further review …

Inside every rule, there is a "spirit." In football, for example, the NFL rulebook is 135 pages+/- with ARs (approved rulings) serving as written illustrations of a rule. Further, a casebook has some 200+ examples to help clarify a rule. Wouldn't it be simpler just to say—please play with the common-good in mind? Too simplistic, huh?

In recent NFL games, players have "faked" injuries to stop the clock without using a time-out or causing a penalty to gain an advantage. It gets complicated to detail how to stop the clock for an injured player—but let's try. Since each T*E*A*M is allowed three time-outs per half, what if a team has exhausted its time-outs and a player becomes injured, then what? If it's prior to the last two minutes of the second or fourth quarters, it's a non-issue—just stop the clock and remove the injured player, who must stay out of the game for at least one play.

After the two-minute notification, in the second or fourth quarter, with the offensive team having exhausted its timeouts and a player of that team becoming injured, the referee shall "runoff" 10 seconds before the ball is made ready for play. If a defensive player is injured and must be removed, no 10-second runoff is required. But, back to that "fake" injury referred to earlier.

Feigning an injury has been around a long time. The rule was installed, when it became apparent that an offensive team was using it to beat the stopping-of-the-clock rule. Should game officials decide if a player is *really* injured? Absolutely not, says rule 4, section 5, article 2, AR 4.71. Moreover, "The rules committee depreciates (love that word) feigning injuries, with subsequent withdrawal of a player to obtain a time-out without a penalty. Coaches are urged to cooperate in discouraging this practice," says rule 4, section 5, article 5, supplemental note 4. Clear enough?

Rules are designed to protect players. However, if game officials are prohibited from determining an injury, how does an administrative staff make such determination? The spirit of *every* rule lies on the shoulders of *every* player, *every* coach, and *every* official. That spirit must prevail.

 Will you follow the spirit of the rule beyond its written word?

January 23, 2012

After further review …

Boundaries—we all have and need them, yet how often, and why, do some people infringe on another's? Perhaps one explanation is that of not respecting the other person's space—or maybe it's the offender's lack of self-respect. When people have "whelming" (versus overwhelming or underwhelming), i.e., a balance in their lives, they respect another's space—call it dignity and honor.

When football players violate a boundary, a foul is called. Using the line of scrimmage (LOS), as an example, each T*E*A*M has its own LOS and the space between those two lines is called the "neutral zone." When a player illegally enters that NZ, it is called a "neutral zone infraction" (NZI) or an "offsides" (OOF), and a foul is called by an official. In life, we all have our neutral zones, which is the space that belongs to each of us. When a person's neutral zone is violated, there is usually not an official around to "flag" that violation. Or is there? Stay tuned.

If one steals some else's property, that crime is punishable by law, if the stealer (no relation to Pittsburgh) is caught and found guilty. Although we all have been taught right from wrong, some believe they won't be caught. It's not the penalty of which we should be wary, but the mere fact that we didn't do the right thing. On the field, there are officials whose responsibility is to enforce those who don't do the right thing. On the other hand, who's "on duty" in the home? Stay tuned.

The recent alleged sexual molestations involving sports figures are boundary issues—addiction notwithstanding. Those who witness such happenings, e.g., child molestations, domestic violence, etc., now become the referees. Their responsibility is to report it (a legal must) to authorities—a major issue in the Sandusky case. Additionally, our military is now reporting sexual assaults into the thousands.

To learn about these issues, as well as one's responsibility, you are encouraged to attend a screening of a film called *Boyhood Shadows*, followed by a panel discussion of what to look for and what to do about it. The event is tonight at MPC Lecture Forum 103 from 6:00 to 8:00 p.m.—admission free. I will be there to moderate a panel of experts. For more information, call (831) 373-3955.

 Will you "stand up" or "stand by" when witnessing sexual violence?

After further review …

"Catch people doing something right" is a phrase I often use, challenging audiences to help them build self-confidence in others, as well as a way to improve T*E*A*M building. That phrase is a gift from my mentor and colleague Dr. Ken Blanchard of *One Minute Manager* fame. A noted author and speaker, Blanchard is a great "cheerleader" (as he calls himself) in helping people grow and work together.

Moving forward … the media seem to enjoy promoting the negative by finding something adverse in those who fail to perform as expected. In the world of sports, for example, a recent headline was titled "Toothless Tiger falters again," when Tiger Woods had a bad day in the final round of the 2012 AT&T Pebble Beach Pro-Am. Tiger didn't shy from media interviews following that tournament when he said, As good as I felt on the greens yesterday (Saturday) is as bad as I felt today (Sunday)." He shot a 75 on that final day.

This is not to defend Tiger, per se, but to point out that the media seem to enjoy highlighting the failures of athletes. Is this approach meant for selling the news? Should this type of reporting take precedent over good when it happens? The press, however, did emphasize the success of golfer Phil Mickelson, who came from six shots back on Sunday to win. Still, the media doesn't want to let go of the "bad blood" that at one time existed between those two. While there may have been a strained relationship in the past, it was quickly put to rest in these post-tournament interviews.

"I enjoy playing with Tiger, since he does bring out the best in me" said Mickelson in his press conference. Tiger countered with "I've always enjoyed playing with Phil; his wedge game was right on the money today." Sounds like both athletes are following that expression: "Catch people doing something right." True competitors need to welcome competition with a healthy attitude—that's what makes, or should make, sports a wholesome sight. Although these two golfers have different personalities in their play, we need to accept them as they are. Furthermore, this phrase applies in the home, the classroom, the office, and most of life's endeavors.

What are your thoughts about catching people doing something right?

After further review …

For 31 years, my responsibility on the NFL field was to ensure justice with integrity. It was never important to me which T*E*A*M won or lost, but that the game was played fairly and within the rules. The same principle held true on the campus in my role as a teacher and principal. Justice had to be meted out fairly.

With the understanding that young people need guidance, support, and encouragement, it was my task to see that they were honest in their reporting of an untoward incident. Yes, youngsters do find ways to manipulate the facts to "cover their tracks." These are mostly learned, not inherent, tendencies that they have witnessed in their elders. So, when I read of Brian Banks recently walking out of the courtroom a free man with his head held high, I was elated, but terribly upset.

In 2002, Banks was arrested and charged with rape. Allegedly Banks, a promising high school football star, dragged a female classmate into a school stairwell and had forcible sex with her. Faced with the possibility of a 40-years-to-life sentence, Banks' lawyer persuaded him to accept a plea deal that put him behind bars for 62 months, to be followed by five years of probation. The remainder of his life would be lived as a registered sex offender, branded with an electronic ankle monitor. His dreams of playing college, and hopefully professional, football shattered.

Once released from prison, Banks was "friended" on Facebook by Wanetta Gibson, who said she made up the rape charge and admitted that what happened was consensual. Gibson's family had sued the Long Beach school district and won a $1.5 million dollar settlement. Where is the justice for Banks?

The proliferation of child molestation cases today is beyond anything expected in a civilized society. The damage done to the victims is tragic and lifelong. Given the nature of sexual assault cases, we tend to side with the victims. But justice must serve both sides.

How does Banks deal with the injustice he suffered? His chances of a pro football career have pretty much disappeared. However, enrolling himself in a community college or even a four-year school to continue his education, and, perhaps, play football at that level is a plausible solution. Given the hand he was dealt, it is important that he "move on" and put the injustice behind him.

 How will you deal with an injustice that may come your way?

9 MENTORING

After further review …

Two prominent sports stars are in the spotlight as I write this: Santonio Holmes and Michael Phelps—both for the wrong reasons. Holmes caught the winning touchdown pass with 35 seconds left in Super Bowl XLIII that sealed the Pittsburgh Steelers' sixth Super Bowl title as they defeated the Arizona Cardinals 27-23.

Holmes' catch was certainly a sensational "feat' of athleticism and he was rewarded by being named Super Bowl XLVIII MVP. Holmes has had his share of off-field problems, and during the 2008 season, Steelers' head coach Mike Tomlin deactivated him for one game. Holmes was arrested and charged with possession of a small amount of marijuana. Small amount? Sorta like being "a little bit pregnant."

Where was his focus and sense of loyalty to his T.E.A.M. during the season? By the way, that game for which Holmes was suspended, the Steelers lost to the New York Giants. The Giants, of course, had their own issues during the 2008 season with WR Plaxico Burress, who was arrested—and suspended—for shooting himself in the leg with a gun he was not licensed to carry. What happened to "just do the right thing?" As we say in my book, "It's the will, not the skill."

Holmes says he's "learned his lesson" and was given cogitative advice from teammate Hines Ward, who told Holmes (when he won the MVP) to "stay humble." Holmes spent his time after the Super Bowl game with his three young kids watching a movie. Good for him.

Phelps, winner of eight gold medals for the USA in the 2008 Olympics held in Beijing, was photographed inhaling from a marijuana pipe (bong) in November 2008 at a party. Phelps, who attributes his swimming prowess to his superior training and conditioning, obviously lost his focus on what got him to the pinnacle of success.

Phelps appeared almost daily in the news apologizing for his "regrettable behavior," which has now cost him the loss of sponsorships, as well as esteem. Further, the USA Swimming Committee suspended him for three months. While it is admirable that Phelps is remorseful, the "role model" tag, as envisioned here, is the athlete who says "no way" and thus avoids situations like these in the first place.

Some have proclaimed both Holmes and Phelps as heroes for their athletic accomplishments. Heroes? Not in my book. Role models? Hopefully, only if their future behavior is unequivocal, and casts a positive influence on others.

Will your behavior reflect yourself as a role model, rather than focusing on sports "heroes"?

May 3, 2010

After further review …

A recent visitor to our home is a friend and former NFL official. We'd been friends for 30+ years, when he joined the ranks of NFL officiating. He was a top college official and a very successful businessman, eventually owning his own company. However, as a rookie official, he had a lot to learn—all rookies do.

During the time I was an NFL referee (crew chief/white hat), the NFL supervisor often assigned a rookie to our crew; I liked that. My reason was two-fold: 1) I enjoyed the opportunity to teach new officials; and 2) I wanted to learn from them. You see, as one ages, it's easy to rely on what you've done over the years. A new official may bring a fresh idea of mechanics (positioning on the field) and/or rules interpretation.

The aforementioned was a large part of the discussion (I'll call him) "Bob" and I had during that visit. Bob was very complimentary to me, saying how much he was thankful for my guidance and nurturing. He was overly complimentary. My response to those kind words was "That's what I do." Now, before you get the idea that this is about self-aggrandizement, let me make this point.

In my book, *Impartial Judgment*, I devoted a chapter titled "We all need mentors—and I've had the best." I learned early in life to associate myself with those who are smarter and more experienced than I. It has served me well. As I grew in knowledge and wisdom, it became my turn to help others—thus the expression, "That's what I do."

If you subscribe to the theory of "the law of attraction," then you understand that what you think about and believe in is what you attract; when you attract those new thoughts and ideas, you begin to assimilate them into who you are; thus, "That's what I do."

That philosophy has served me well over my years as a referee, teacher, and school administrator, as well as my recent privilege as a college trustee. Once an individual understands that life and its experiences are not about him/her, but merely an opportunity to be a "lamplighter," then "that's what I do" happens. The rewards, if they are to come, are the occasions to bask in the satisfaction of watching others grow.

As someone once said, "Life is not measured by the number of breaths we take, but by the number of moments that take our breath away." Nurturing others creates those moments.

 Will you be a giver and/or teacher/mentor to others?

August 2, 2010

After further review …

"Proud" doesn't begin to express my feelings as I watched Doug Harvey being inducted into the Major League baseball 2010 class Hall of Fame in Cooperstown, New York. Proud because Harvey is my friend and has been for 55 years. As I listened to his wonderful induction speech, I recalled the history that he and I had.

Harv and I officiated high school, junior college, and college basketball games together in Southern California. We shared those officiating times with Darrell Garretson, who later went on to officiate 27 years in the NBA and followed that as NBA Supervisor of Officials. I learned a lot from those two.

First and foremost, that we all love the game, whether it be baseball, basketball, or football, and loved officiating. Harv said it well in his induction speech, "It is our job to protect the integrity of the game—to see that every play, every game, is played fairly." It was not important to Harv who won the game, but that it was won by the rules.

Second, he said it was important to know the rules of the game, and not just the written rules, but the sense of what is right. Study of those rules took time and effort— "two hours every day," Harv said, as was climbing the ladder to the Major Leagues, where he worked 4,673 games in 31 years.

Most importantly, Harv thanked his dad, "as my idol," who provided him guidance, inspiration, and encouragement. I feel similarly about my dad. The support of parents and family is vital to success. The old saw "self-made man" (or woman) is specious. No one makes it by him or herself. Harv's words about his father rang loudly in my ears as my dad was my first—and most respected—mentor.

As we proceed on our journey, lessons learned from our colleagues become vital to our success. In my book, *Impartial Judgment*, I devoted a chapter to mentorinig, saying, "We all need mentors, and I had the best." Harv, in his induction speech, gave credit to many who provided him incentive and encouragement. Growing, improving, getting better each time, each game, is important to be at one's best every time.

Harv also felt it important that he "carry the torch" to mentor younger officials, not only his crew (as crew chief), but to anyone who sought his counsel. A number of those attended that Hall of Fame induction to honor and to say "thanks" to their mentor.

 Will you accept mentoring with enough gratitude to pass on to others?

After further review …

The Jackie Robinson biopic, directed by Brian Helgeland and just released by Warner Bros., is a story that will reach deep into your soul. The world it inhabits is baseball, America's erstwhile national pastime. But it is far more than a baseball film; it's a story about human beings *for* human beings. The film uses baseball and Jackie Robinson as vehicles to describe the struggle of an African-American player being integrated into what was then an "all white-man's game."

Branch Rickey (played by Harrison Ford), the Brooklyn Dodgers' president and GM, was the force behind the inclusion of the first black player in Major League baseball. Scrutinizing the Negro league, Rickey searched for a candidate who could not only play the game at the highest professional level, but could also withstand the degradation and humiliation that would inevitably occur. He chose Robinson (played by Chadwick Boseman), born in Georgia, but raised in Pasadena, California. After attending and starring in four sports at Pasadena Junior College, Robinson had been a successful and superlative athlete at UCLA.

The film begins in August, 1945, the year he was signed by Rickey to a Minor League contract in Montreal. However, I had met Jack Roosevelt Robinson in the fall of 1937. My dad, Jim Sr., refereed many junior college football games, quite often in the Rose Bowl where PJC played. Carrying dad's officiating bag, we would simply walk through the gate (security being almost non-existent), down the ramp, and into the officials' dressing room. When the crew of four would emerge, I walked with them onto the Rose Bowl field and sat on the home team's (PJC) bench.

I clearly remember dad approaching me at halftime one game and saying, "Now just watch this colored boy play; he's really something," as he pointed to Jackie. (Remember that this was 1937 and "colored" was considered an acceptable term for African Americans in that era.) Dad, who earlier that decade had been Kenny Washington's football coach at Lincoln High School in Los Angeles and helped him get into UCLA (where he later played in the same backfield with Jackie), had nothing but respect for them both. As I followed Jackie's career through UCLA and into the Dodgers' organization, I'm proud to say he became part of my heritage.

Each April 15th, every MLB player wears the number 42 in tribute to a player I met when he was a teenager. What a fortunate circumstance.

 Will you seek out others who may provide you with a model that you can emulate?

After further review …

The despicable plight of Aaron Hernandez, erstwhile tight end of the New England Patriots, has overtaken sports headlines around the country. Too bad that negative news of athletes supplants the good things so many of our professional athletes do.

Hernandez, a talented football star (famously paired with Rob Gronkowski, the Patriots' other Pro Bowl end), is being held without bail on murder charges. Hernandez allegedly shot a friend (Odin Lloyd) and disposed of his body in an industrial park. He is also under investigation for other gun-related crimes in Massachusetts and Florida. He is said to have expressed a desire to get married while in solitary confinement. It may be less true love than a means by which his fiancé wouldn't be compelled to testify.

My intent here is not so much to focus on Hernandez, but to point out that 3,000 other professional football players will be starting training camp this month, preparing for the 2013 season. Each of the 32 NFL teams will bring some 100 elite athletes to camp, and then carefully select the 53 who will compose the game roster of each T*E*A*M.

How special is that? Statistics suggest that there are some 30 felons among those 3,000 prospects, or .01 percent. Those same 30 distributed among 1,700 who make up the final rosters pushes the rate to 1.1111 percent, a more troubling figure. The NFL has had programs in place for many years to help guide incoming and present players who are confronted with money and status issues. Further, athletes have representation committed to their best interests. Yet, that guidance doesn't always "take."

With the dropout rate in the American educational system hovering in the 40 to 50 percent range, we can't expect its performance and behavior standards to be universally absorbed. But ethical and practical guidance does exist for those who can see beyond instant gratification. Is that what leered Hernandez into dysfunction? Or was it the seduction of DYKWIAM (Don't You Know Who I am)?

What is most important here is how to enable our athletes to avoid these potholes. Perhaps a program called Transformational Coaching, now springing up here on the California Central Coast, could be of service. TCCC is a program designed to coach young people from the "inside-out," creating the person from within in conjunction with improving their God-given athletic skills. If only this program could have captured Hernandez early on.

 Will you teach/coach/parent your youngster from the inside-out?

10 PERSONAL GROWTH

iStock/Thinkstock

July 12, 2010

After further review …

One of my mentors in the profession of public speaking was W.H. Gove, the first president of the National Speakers Association. Because of our common interest in sports, he and I shared many discussions about athletic talent. We expanded that discussion to talent of all kinds.

Gove stated skills were acquired with these words: "Some things are easy to learn and easy to do—cry; a baby learns without prior knowledge how and when to cry and does it often and easily."

Some things are easy to learn and hard to do: speak—very young children learn to speak in a language spoken to them without a lot of lessons. However, to stand on one's feet and speak effectively with proper use of language is *hard* to do. For many, the fear of speaking in public is greater than the fear of death.

Some things are hard to learn and hard to do: golf—of the millions of golfers, with par at 72, less than one out of five break 100.

Some things are easy to learn and when you can't remember where or when you learned it, Gove says, "That's called *talent*."

This led us to discuss many of our talented sports stars, i.e., not only who they are, but how they got to their level of supremacy. Of the 255 players drafted in the 2010 NFL draft, less than 100 will make final rosters and fewer will last more than four years.

High draft choices often don't make it, e.g., JaMarcus Russell, 2007 first-round pick of the Oakland Raiders (as of this writing) is out of the NFL. Whereas, Tom Brady, drafted #199 by the New England Patriots in 2000, has been three times a Super Bowl champion and two of those as MVP. How does talent get better or worse?

Tim Tebow, drafted 25th by the Denver Broncos this year, after a stellar career (first team All American and 2007 Heisman trophy awardee) at Florida, was quoted recently saying, "Hard work beats talent when talent doesn't work hard." There is no question in this writer's belief that *talent* is God-given. It is foolish to think otherwise.

Having spent 31 years on the NFL field with so many talented athletes, I must wholeheartedly agree with Tebow, to wit: Hard work is what it takes to achieve at the highest level and that applies to whatever we do—not just sports.

 Will you spend the time, energy, study, and practice necessary to achieve your goals?

March 28, 2011

After further review …

During March Madness, a radio interviewer asked a basketball scholar-athlete an interesting question: "What have you learned on the playing court that could help you in the classroom?" Great question. The answer, however, must have caught the athlete, who has a reported 3.75 GPA, by surprise, since his answer was, "I don't know." Let's give that athlete the benefit of the doubt. We all have been asked questions that have caught us off-guard.

The interviewer's question immediately brought to mind the term "transfer of learning." Indeed, there are ideas/tools, etc. that an athlete can use both in the classroom and on the playing field/court. Here are just 10 that quickly come to mind (in no priority order):

1. *Be on time.* No excuses. No exceptions. Many have adopted the Lombardi time rule that just being on time isn't enough. His rule was that a player must be 15 minutes earlier than the appointed time. Being late is disrespectful to your team and classmates, as well as to the leader.

2. *Preparation.* Every player has to be physically, mentally, and spiritually ready in order to practice and play at his best. That applies to the classroom as well.

3. *Focus.* While multitasking is "in" in today's lifestyle, a singleness of purpose helps us achieve our goals more successfully.

4. *Goal(s).* Football, as an example, is a game of goals with the ultimate purpose to cross the goal line. Setting academic goals gives us a "rudder" to steer toward achievement.

5. *Self-confidence.* Believing in your abilities starts and must continue with you. "If it's to be, it's up to me" is an expression to be repeated often.

6. *Don't quit.* Never give up. The possibilities always lie ahead of you, not behind you. Keep hope alive.

7. *Mental toughness.* When the game is on-the-line, you need to rely on your inner strengths that you will make it happen.

8. *Do the right thing.* There are no shortcuts to being honest and trustworthy. Your integrity will serve you well.

9. *T*E*A*M—Together Everyone Accomplishes More.* No such thing as a "self-made man." Don't be afraid to ask for help. We all need others to help us succeed.

10. *Never be completely satisfied.* There is always more to accomplish.

 Will you add to this list things you can use to transfer learning?

After further review …

On May 9, 2011, Frank Chirkinian was inducted into the World Golf Hall of Fame in St. Augustine, Florida. This induction was long overdue and held posthumously, with Frank having succumbed to cancer on March 4, 2011.

Chirkinian was called many names in his life: master storyteller, Michelangelo, best-there-ever-was, entertainer, competitor, genius, and to some, "Ayatollah." He was all those things. To me, however, he was simply a "friend." The dictionary never will have enough words to express my feelings for Frank.

We met in the 1960s when Frank was a CBS producer of NFL games and I was a referee. The TV producer would visit the referees prior to the game to review commercial breaks and other TV issues. It was always a pleasure to see Frank walk into our dressing room, as I knew that the telecast would be in good hands, and moreover, there was no question about who would be "in charge." Some years later, we reconnected when Frank was producing golf—always his first love—for "The Crosby" in Pebble Beach. It was then that our relationship grew to a lifelong friendship.

During that week in Pebble Beach, I would invite Frank and his talented crew of announcers for dinner in our home, and he would invite me to sit in the CBS truck to watch him and his staff masterfully craft every golf shot. Frank was, indeed, a visionary. He knew what a viewer, golfer or not, wanted to see. For example, Frank put into the place the red versus black scoring system so the viewers knew how far out in front the leader was and how far back the challengers were. Today, we just take that for granted.

Chirkinian put a camera in the blimp so that viewers could see what a course of 7000+ yards the golfer was facing. Although golf is played in a quiet (shhh!) environment, on-course spectators can hear the club hitting the ball—an exciting sound. Frank put microphones on the tee boxes so viewers at home could "feel" the action, as if they were there. Frank was, indeed, in show business—not just sports—as he commanded "18 live stages" every year from his CBS truck, including 38 consecutive Masters.

 Will Chirkinian's poetry-in-action inspire you to think differently about what you do?

After further review …

Ever had a bad day? Sure you have. If you can't recall that "bad day," well, maybe you have succeeded in blocking it from your data base (i.e., memory bank). Or maybe you just never had one, it just happened. Not having a bad day is not necessarily a good thing, since strong character is often built from difficult experiences—if and when you move on.

Vin Mazzaro, a relief pitcher for the Kansas City Royals (not a household name in MLB), had one of those "bad days" this 2011 season. Mazzaro gave up 14—yes 14—earned runs in relief in just two innings, the fourth and fifth, in a game against the Cleveland Indians. That many earned runs happens in Little League baseball, but, certainly not in MLB. Well, it did happen and has happened before, but not since 1919—92 years ago.

Other pitchers in MLB have given up that many runs (14), including Bob Feller, but no one did it like Mazzaro in just two and one-third innings. Some of the blame might be credited to Royals' manager Ned Yost, who didn't want to decimate his bullpen by using all his relief staff. But as "Annie" always says, "The sun'll come tomorrow, bet your bottom dollar, there'll be sun." Well, the sun did come up the next day and when it did, Mazzaro was on a bus to Papillion (a suburb of Omaha, NE), as he was "sent down" to the Royals' AAA T*E*A*M, the Omaha Storm Chasers.

This essay is not so much about Mazzaro, who at 24 may have had his most embarrassing day on the mound, but more about how to deal with a setback. First and foremost, is that help can be sought. We need to encourage others not to be afraid of saying, "I need help"—especially our young people. Suicide is the second leading cause of death among our youth. Others around someone in need must "step up" to help. There is no one among us who does not need help in difficult times.

Coach Herm Edwards reminds us that "you can lose your momentum, but *never* lose your confidence." Self-confidence and a belief that "this too will pass" can help us move on. Mazzaro will be back one day.

 Will you help others in their time of need?

After further review ...

As the nation celebrates the birthday of Dr. Martin Luther King Jr., I vividly recall his "I have a dream ..." speech in August, 1963. Dr. King was only 34 at the time. During that month/year, I was officiating in the NFL and remember the tensions on the field between black and white players. Colorblindness hadn't progressed much in the early 60s. Some progress has been made 48 years later.

Dr. King's speech was about "acceptance" of others—meaning all people. The sports world has made a good deal of progress in this area. A black offensive guard working alongside a white offensive tackle must never consider the color of his teammate to create a successful outcome.

First, for a T*E*A*M to create a winning climate, it must have harmony. Coaches call it chemistry, which promotes the idea that the team comes first and "I" am only a part of it. Tebow (Denver Broncos' quarterback) comes to mind—should we place harmony with Tebowing? Drew Brees (New Orleans Saints' quarterback), recently setting a single season passing record of 5,084 yards, said it loud and clear—"This is not about one guy, this is about all of us working together."

Second, each player must believe in his abilities, as well as that of his teammates—call it optimism. Fans' signs saying "We Believe" appeared many times in support of their teams. While it may be trite (trite because it is true), failure is not getting knocked down; failure is not getting back up after being knocked down. Ya gotta believe!

Third, as was said in last week's Tunney Side regarding setting goals, there must a pathway. The lack of a pathway, i.e., goals, is like a ship without a rudder; there is difficulty staying on course. Write down what you want to accomplish, and then follow that path.

And finally, you can't do it alone—everyone is important to a team's success. The collective strength of everyone will always be stronger than any single individual. Closing your hand to make a fist gives strength to each of its parts—called fingers (try it).

Combining these four words—Harmony, Optimism, Pathway, and Everyone—creates the acronym HOPE, which is what Dr. King's dream was designed to be. Keep HOPE alive.

 Will you use HOPE as your guide in your next endeavor?

After further review …

As we begin a new year, we need to decide for ourselves if we want merely to be successful or to strive for the significance that my friend and colleague Dan Clark (danclarkspeak.com) advocates. Clark says successful people get what they want and can win on any given day, but those who live lives of significance want what they get by creating dynasties that can outlast them. In his powerful, upcoming book *The Act of Significance—Achieving the Level Beyond Success,* Clark tells of a teammate who was an NFL second-round draft pick, but who quit after four years. He liked being a football player, but hated playing football. He got what he wanted, but hated what he had to do to get it.

Clark challenges our belief systems by replacing lower preparatory principles with what he calls the "Twelve Highest Universal Laws of Life-Changing Leadership" that champions obey. For example, Clark teaches that patience is overrated, reinforcing passivity, allowing us never to begin. Perseverance is the higher law, presupposing that we will take our turn, and thus see the result of our effort. It is not enough to say "I will do my best." We must succeed at doing that which is necessary.

We certainly have an example with the Indianapolis Colts, who began their 2012 season with a rookie quarterback (Andrew Luck) after losing one of the best-ever quarterbacks. While rookie quarterbacks usually do not have a running start at a successful first year, Luck and his teammates did, without their head coach Chuck Pagano, who was diagnosed with leukemia in September, 2012 and forced to take a leave of absence. The Colts rallied behind their stricken coach, many players shaving their heads in solidarity with him as he underwent chemotherapy. Thus motivated, the Colts made it to the playoffs. This is a case of significance trumping success.

The book spoke clearly to me. Its key message is about going beyond ordinary measurements of success, by helping others transform their lives/thinking/being to overcome difficulties they may be facing. The value beyond personal gain, *significance*, is the keystone to the building blocks of successful teamwork. How often have we seen sports stars attain success via their athletic prowess, yet fail to show compassion and concern for their families or society? Real happiness follows from identifying and striving for the higher level of significance. This book will change the way you lead, manage, coach, or parent.

 Will you confront the challenge that Clark presents in his book?

After further review …

"Ac-Cent-Tchu-Ate the Positive!" Johnny Mercer's beloved standard ruled the optimistic roost until "What a Wonderful World" (written by Bob Thiele, recorded by Louis Armstrong) came along in 1967. And though both classics have the whiff of antiquity now, we still see examples of positive attitude every day. This writer may have recently chastised movie and sports stars for their egregious behavior, but there are many others who are "Wonderful World" role models. As an example, take Ashton Kutcher, star of the popular sitcom "Two and a Half Men."

Kutcher recently spoke to a teenage audience at the Teen Choice awards. I watched that speech and later saw him interviewed on a talk show where he reiterated his approach to life. Kutcher said, "I believe that opportunity looks a lot like hard work. I've never had a job in my life that I was better than. I was always just lucky to have a job. And every job I had was a stepping stone to my next job, and I never quit my job until I had my next job. The sexiest thing in the entire world is being smart and being thoughtful and being generous."

I can hear former coach and current ESPN analyst Herm Edwards saying the same thing. I can hear NFL stars Larry Fitzgerald, Robert Griffin III, and the Manning brothers (Peyton and Eli) echoing this message to teenagers. Many sports stars are sincere with their positive messages and generous with their time and energy helping others.

The teenagers cheered loudly for Kutcher, their attention captured by the "sexy" energy of his message. But will they heed those words by following that advice into action? In the sales world, we say, "Nothing happens until somebody sells something." Kutcher laid down a challenge before those kids: You'll be lucky to have a job; don't take anything for granted.

The millennium generation often seems stuck on the concept of *entitlement*. That may be coloring them with too broad a brush, but an important lesson that Kutcher and the sports stars are providing for them is that *nothing comes for free*. There is no guarantee of the result. It's one's effort, perseverance, and desire that are needed to reach success. It helps, along that path, to "E-lim-i-nate the Negative" and "Don't Mess with Mr. In-Between" (thanks Mr. Mercer).

 Will you design your path with smartness, thoughtfulness, and generosity?

11 SUCCESS

After further review …

The Secret, a book on the best seller list with the movie of the same name, explains the law of attraction. Simply stated, the law of attraction says you will attract what you think about and/or how you think about something. If you think something won't work or can't be achieved, it's more likely that it won't. Therefore, when you want something good or positive to happen, the law of attraction indicates it more likely will. No guarantees, and that's what makes life interesting.

Napoleon Hill, the author of *Think and Grow Rich*, wrote, "What the mind can conceive, and believe, it can achieve." The operative word is "believe." So often, we conceive (think about) what we want, and, maybe even are strong in our thoughts, but then, the negative pops into our mind, "But what if I fail?" Zappo, you probably will, because you edged out "believe." Sports give us the visible examples of believing. A player intently focused on a goal is said to be in the "zone," thereby attracting what that player wants to happen.

I once asked an Olympic high jumper what he was thinking about in his preparation before starting his run toward the bar. He said, "I visualize myself launching my body overt the bar and landing in the pit." "Well," I said, "don't you ever picture yourself knocking off the bar with your elbow or foot?" "Never," he responded. "Why would you picture failure?" That's the "secret." You attract what you think about. Yet, often, we let "what if?" disrupt our positive intention.

This concept is not new. Dean Cromwell, former University of Southern California track coach called all of his athletes "champ." "Hi, champ, how you doing?" "See you at practice today, champ." What the coach was doing was planting the word "champ" in the mind of each of each of his athletes, thereby helping them to attract success by thinking and believing they were champions.

To be a champion, you must think—and believe—you are and can be that person you want to be. In today's sports world, that idea sometimes gets overplayed when athletes proclaim they are bigger than the sport. "Meism" takes that concept of "champ" too far. When that happens, the letter "u" replaces the "a" and we get "chump."

The law of attraction works in anything you do—learning, teaching, selling, managing, etc. As an example, if you want your business to succeed, you must believe that it will. You will attract what you think about.

 Will you attract success by believing in what you want to happen?

After further review …

During a recent conversation I had with the executive director of the AT&T Pebble Beach Junior Golf Association, she was discussing the nine core values their junior golfers (ages 7-17) can learn from the great game of golf and further, put into practice in their daily lives: *respect, honesty, integrity, sportsmanship, confidence, responsibility, perserverance, courtesy,* and *judgment*. She said she was proud to be part of such a program.

The AT&T Pebble Beach Junior Golf Association is 25-years young and preceded, maybe even gave impetus to, the nationwide First Tee movement. This junior golf program has 60 golf professionals on the Monterey (California) Peninsula providing lessons, clinics, tournaments, and scholarships for some 1,300 junior golfers. The cost to these kids is an annual fee of $25. Golf clubs, hats, and balls are provided free of charge for any financially-challenged player. Tournament competition occurs within five age divisions (platinum, gold, silver, bronze, and copper).

She was effusive in describing how remarkable the character of these youngsters is. Then she related a story about a young golfer who had finished a tournament third in his division. When he returned home he held his medallion up disgustedly and said to his father, "Look, all I got was this dumb medal." It may be an isolated case, but how could any kid be ungrateful for finishing third? Is first place the only reward? Surely, there is a lesson to be learned here.

I wondered how his father responded. The opportunity to help an unhappy golfer overcome his disappointment could be crucial to the boy's future, since dealing with unfulfilled expectations will always be part of his life. As the ancient Greek philosopher Epicurus said, "It's not what happens to you, but how you react to it that matters." Now, this young man probably couldn't care less about Epicurus, but those nine core values can certainly help him. There are many ways a parent, coach, or teacher can be of positive benefit in these situations.

Oh, BTW, that aforementioned executive director is Linda Tunney, my wife, who for 18 years has been in charge of this valuable program. The Junior Golf Association does so much for these kids, not the least of which is introducing them to those nine core values. Linda was recently inducted in the PGA Hall of Fame, Monterey Bay Chapter, for her service to the game of golf and to young people. Way to go, Hon!

 Will your service to others be of Hall of Fame caliber?

After further review …

The Academy of Motion Picture Arts and Sciences recently presented Oscars for the "best" motion picture, "best" director, "best" actor/actress, and numerous other categories, during its 85th awards show. I have seen the work of most nominees and I am not a critic, yet I always struggle with the concept of "best." You may well ask what that has to do with sports; isn't that what this column/blog concerns itself with? Indeed it is, and Tunney Side is now in its eighth year of taking a closer look at current sports stories and issues, with the goal of reframing them in a way that reinforces and strengthens a positive view of everyday life. Stay tuned.

One question is regularly asked of me: who was the "best" NFL player you shared the field with during your 31 years as an NFL referee? You can understand my apprehension toward that term. Just as the Oscars always represent a subjective judgment, it's only fair to say that judging an athlete is subjective as well. To be sure those inducted into the Pro Football Hall of Fame (the Oscar of football, as it were) have hard-earned stats and numbers on their side. And yet, there is always a question of who's the best, and the answer is inevitably subjective.

The 2013 Pro Football H of F class is well deserving of this honor. Still, many other deserving candidates were pushed into future voting or discarded as others became eligible. If you consider that there are only 1700 athletes playing in the NFL in any given year, you realize these are the best of an enormous pool of men wearing pads. So how do you choose the "best-of-the-best?" Many ancillary factors, such as the era, T*E*A*M components, style of play, and competitive balance must be taken into consideration.

However, what stood out most dramatically for me during that Academy Award ceremony was the gratitude expressed by actor/director/producer Ben Affleck in his acceptance speech for the movie "Argo." He said, "So many people extended themselves to me when I couldn't get a job. You have to work harder than you think you possibly can … it doesn't matter how you get knocked down in life, 'cause that's gonna happen. All that matters is that you gotta get up." In the Tunney Side's view, that is the key to achieving one's best.

 Will you strive to be at your best when your best is required?

After further review …

The classic expression "the whole is greater than the sum of its parts" has always made sense to me. These "Tunney Side" essays, along with my presentations to corporate and business groups, have consistently emphasized the word T*E*A*M: "Together Everyone Accomplishes More." That message, which I often employ, was brought home to me during an NFL officiating crew's devotional service, which took place on a recent Sunday morning prior to the game they were working.

The devotional leader shared the writings of Will Graham, grandson of the iconic evangelist Billy Graham, who makes the comparison of a human body's composition with that of an NFL team. Will asserts that God very carefully created each human so that one body part is dependent on all the others. When one part is ailing, Will's thesis continues, it affects other parts; he observed that when one player on a team is injured, the other players respectfully "take-a-knee" in prayer for the recovery of the injured.

Will reminds us to value each other by emphasizing that in football it is important that all 11 men take the field together. However, if only two or three arrive on the field to play while the others hang back on the bench, that team cannot accomplish its purpose. Will's analogy, the devotional leader said, not only applies to his crew of seven officials, but to the family, a company, or any organization—*each of us needs all of us.*

Will's theme stresses the interdependence of each member. A cornerback, for example, depends upon his defensive line to put pressure on the quarterback, just as each of our body parts depends on another. Our eyes supply us with one vital stream of information while our fingers do their job in a different sense-realm, yet one suffers or must compensate if the other malfunctions. In an officiating crew, the responsibilities of the judge differ from those of the referee, yet each must perform at the top level for the crew to perform effectively.

In the family, trustworthy relationships with other family members grow from our concern for each other. In the NFL teams I have watched over the course of many years, this caring relationship has created successful mutual accomplishments, the benefits of which last long after playing days are over.

 Will you apply Will's philosophy to your T*E*A*M?

After further review …

My Alhambra High School (CA) principal, Dr. Norm Scherer, would often remind our student body that "about 2 percent of you are misbehaving and giving our school a bad name." He went on to say that it was up to 100 percent of us to maintain proper behavior on and off campus. He didn't use the word "implode" (to burst inward), but the more modern term was implicit in his caution.

In today's world, it seems to happen to many seeking fame. Lindsay Lohan (27) in and out of legal trouble and rehab; Amanda Bynes (27) with a stretch of bad behavior; Justin Bieber (19); Britney Spears (31); each with well-publicized wrong turns. The list goes on. Is that 2 percent number greater in young people with careers who are in show business?

Many sports stars also implode: Adam "Pacman" Jones, with his violent misadventures in Las Vegas; Michael Vick in his dog-fighting days; and Johnny "Football" Manziel and his obvious string of poor decisions. Is it fame and huge sums of money that lure stars into egregious behavior? How can it be corrected?

The answer can be found in good parenting. Unfortunately, that isn't the background of many celebrities. Sometimes, as was the case at my high school, individuals deliberately turn away from strong, clear guidance, if it gets no confrontation at home. A large number of suddenly wealthy performers and athletes come from disadvantaged environments or, perhaps, single-parent homes. But that doesn't mean a positive example can't be achieved.

The expression "You can take the boy outa the 'hood,' but you can't take the 'hood' outa the boy," doesn't have to be a truism. There are numerous great examples of those who have reached beyond negative early environments to become good citizens. In the absence of good parents, mentors abound. We all need mentors. How about the sport stars' agents? Unfortunately, many agents work to get their clients the best salary possible, but fail to take the time or interest to guide them on a safe path toward personal success.

The keys to a long, healthy career, it seems here, are to surround oneself with positive influences, to listen, and to make smart choices. The good news is many are doing that. Unfortunately, it's that 2 percent that hogs all the publicity.

Will you recognize and heed the wisdom of those who can help you be truly successful in life?

12 TEAMWORK

iStock/Thinkstock

After further review …

Stephen Covey, author of *Seven Habits of Effective People, and The 8th Habit: From Effectiveness to Greatness*, teaches three guidelines for effective collaboration—read: TEAMWORK.

They are: 1) establish your mission; 2) set the ground rules; and 3) identify each member's strengths. Nothing new here. However, it recalled for me how the NFL officiating crew of seven, of which I was the "crew chief," strived to be more effective (read: perfect) on the field every game. See how these apply to you and how you can utilize them each day.

Establish your mission. My book *Impartial Judgment* could have been titled *Cause I Don't Care Who Wins*. The mission of each NFL crew is to officiate *all* 60 minutes of every game without prejudice and mistake-free. Does this put extra pressure on each member of the crew? Not necessarily. Pressure keeps one focused and can be managed when everyone is prepared—mentally and physically. The questions are: a) did each do his homework thoroughly by studying the rulebook? And b) did everyone physically work out each day to be in game condition?

Set the ground rules. Each week, before the next game, every official—by himself, as well as with his crew, studies the game film of their previous week's game, looking for ways to improve. Each crew member must be honest to admit a blown call, a missed play, and that he was not in the right position to make the call (called mechanics). Only when officials learn from their mistakes will improvement take place. These ground rules help the crew seek perfection. Another important ground rule is to be professional on the field—friendly and courteous, but not "buddy-buddy" with players or coaches.

Identify each member's strengths. It is vital that each official is placed in an on-field position (e.g., R, U, HL, LJ, SJ, FJ, or BJ), which utilizes his physical and mental strengths to the utmost. While the major responsibility of enforcing the penalty for a foul, for example, is placed on the referee (white hat), it is essential for the effectiveness of the crew, and of course for the game itself, that every official learn, know, and ensure that every penalty is properly enforced. Finally, while the strength of a crew depends on the strength of the individual, it is the willingness of each to help another T.E.A.M. member. Teamwork—call it chemistry—is crucial to the success of the game.

 Will you practice these suggestions to help your T.E.A.M. move from effectiveness to greatness?

December 20, 2011

After further review …

At this writing, the NBA's Miami Heat is struggling. It was widely expected when LeBron James made his TV narcissistic announcement on ESPN prior to the 2010-11 season that he was leaving the Cleveland Cavaliers to exercise his free agency rights and "take my talents to South Beach," that the Heat would just walk all over the other NBA teams. Hasn't happened.

Sports authorities/experts have known for a long time that talent alone is less apt to win championships than players who will work together effectively. An obvious example of solid T.E.A.M. chemistry is the San Francisco Giants in the MLB—those no-name guys who surprised the baseball world by winning the 2010 World Series. Perhaps, they even surprised themselves.

There was much negativity about what James did—including from this writer. The obvious "maneuvering" that James did to join D. Wade and Chris Bosh was an attempt to "stack the deck." Pro sports can only function as an entity through the draft, the lottery, and trades in order to balance the league. What James did, although he was legally entitled to do so, was to circumvent the NBA's system by putting three superstars together on the same T.E.A.M.

As of this writing, it has not been successful. Each Heat opponent has geared itself to work a little harder. The Heat's opponents seem to play together with a little more T.E.A.M. spirit—called chemistry. Teams do need a superstar, e.g., Michael, Larry, "Magic," Kobe, etc., but individual stars must find a way to work with the others. Can the Heat's three superstars—James, Wade, and Bosh—do that? Can they find that chemistry needed to be world champs?

If I could give you a solid, definitive answer, I'd apply to be the head coach of the Miami Heat. There are some theories, albeit platitudes, which any organization must follow to achieve success/chemistry:

One, they must "buy into" what their coach dictates; two, they must decide on an on-court leader and follow his leadership; three, they must—every game—accept the fact that it is not who scores, but that they (as a T.E.A.M.) score more than their opponent; four, every must play defense, helping his teammate when needed; and five, they must enjoy each other—this can be a fun game when everyone works together.

Will you put your ego aside to help your T.E.A.M. achieve its goal?

ABOUT JIM TUNNEY

Jim Tunney has had an exemplary career in sports. A former high school coach, teacher, principal, and district superintendent, he had a 40-year career in officiating football and basketball. Thirty-one of those years, he was "the face of NFL officiating," working a record twenty-nine post-season games including three Super Bowls (two back-to-back), ten NFC/AFC Championship games, six Pro Bowls, and twenty-five Monday Night games, when MNF was THE game of the week. He officiated some of the most memorable games in NFL history, including "The Ice Bowl," "The Kick," "The Snowball Game," "The Final Fumble," "The Fog Bowl," and "The Catch." His book *IMPARTIAL JUDGMENT: The "Dean of NFL Referees" Calls Pro Football as He Sees It* chronicles his NFL career. Seven times, he has been nominated for the NFL Hall of Fame.

As a professional speaker, he is past president of the National Speakers Association and a charter member of its most prestigious group—The CPAE Speakers Hall of Fame. Jim holds every professional designation of the NSA, including the Philanthropist of the Year and the Cavett—the Oscar of professional speaking.

Dr. Tunney (he received a doctorate in education from the University of Southern California) continues to serve his community as a former headmaster and trustee of York School and former trustee of the Monterey Peninsula College. MPC honored him with its President's Award in 2009. Moreover, that same year he was awarded the Citizen of the Year by the Monterey Chamber of Commerce.

In 1993, he founded the Jim Tunney Youth Foundation to support local community programs that develop leadership, work skills, wellness, and self-esteem in youth. To date, the JTYF has made grants exceeding a quarter million dollars.

He has been inducted into the California Community College Football Hall of Fame and the Multi-Ethnic Sports Hall of Fame, as well as being the first administrator inducted into the Fairfax High School Hall of Fame.

As an author he has written and/or co-authored nine books: *Impartial Judgment; Chicken Soup for the Sports Fan's Soul; Super Bowl Sunday; Speaking Secrets of the Masters; Lessons in Leadership; Insights into Excellence; You Can Do It!; Build a Better You;* and, *It's the Will, Not the Skill.* He continues to write a weekly column for the *Monterey County Herald,* called *On the Tunney Side of Sports.*